Mind Reading
QUICK & EASY

About the Author

Richard Webster is the author of more than fifty titles with Llewellyn, and he is one of New Zealand's most prolific writers. His best-selling books include *Face Reading Quick & Easy*, *Spirit Guides and Angel Guardians*, *Miracles*, and a series of books on feng shui. MagicNZ presented him with a Lifetime Achievement Award for "excellence in writing magical literature" in 2008. His book *Spirit and Dream Animals* received a COVR Award in 2012. In 2013, Richard was made a Grand Master of Magic by the magicians of New Zealand. He has appeared on numerous TV shows including *Hard Copy* and *20/20*. His books have been translated into thirty-one languages.

Mind Reading
QUICK & EASY

Richard Webster

Llewellyn Publications
Woodbury, Minnesota

FIRST EDITION
First Printing, 2015

Book design by Donna Burch-Brown
Cover design by Ellen Lawson
Cover image by iStockphoto.com/26097738/©annebaek
Editing by Stephanie Finne
Interior illustrations by Mary Ann Zapalac

Llewellyn Publishing is a registered trademark of Llewellyn Worldwide Ltd.

Library of Congress Cataloging-in-Publication Data

Webster, Richard, 1946–
  Mind reading quick & easy / Richard Webster. — First Edition.
      pages   cm
  Includes bibliographical references and index.
  ISBN 978-0-7387-4449-0
  1. Telepathy. I. Title. II. Title: Mind reading quick and easy.
  BF1171.W43 2015
  133.8'2—dc23
                                        2014041540

Llewellyn Publications
A Division of Llewellyn Worldwide Ltd.
2143 Wooddale Drive
Woodbury, MN 55125-2989
www.llewellyn.com

Printed in the United States of America

Other Books by Richard Webster

For my good friends
Peter and Judy Withers

Contents

Introduction / 1

1: You Are Already a Mind Reader / 9

2: Everyone Is Different / 15

3: Getting On with Others / 23

4: I Can Read You Like a Book / 39

5: Mind-to-Mind Communication / 63

6: Experiments over the Phone / 83

7: Experiments with Cards / 93

8: More Advanced Experiments / 113

9: Contact Mind Reading / 137

10: Group Tests / 151

11: Interspecies Communication / 163

12: Telepathy in Dreams / 181

13: Telepathy and the Psychic Reader / 195

14: Mind Reading in Everyday Life / 205

Conclusion / 211

Suggested Reading / 213

Index / 219

No one can tell, when two people walk closely together, what
unconscious communication one mind may have with another.
—ROBERT BARR

INTRODUCTION

Have you ever had the experience of knowing who was on the other
end of the phone before you picked up? Do you sometimes know
what someone is going to say before he or she says it? Do you ever
know what someone is really feeling, even when he or she is trying to
conceal it? Have you ever performed a small task and been told, "I was
just going to ask you to do that"? I'm sure you have, as in actuality,
we're all mind readers.

Throughout history, many people have recorded their psychic experiences. A large number of these involve mind-to-mind communication—people receiving the thoughts of others. A well-documented
example of this happened to Bishop Samuel Wilberforce (1805–1873),
a man who was famous for his opposition to Charles Darwin's theory
of evolution.

One day when Bishop Wilberforce was holding a meeting with a
group of clergymen, he suddenly raised a hand to his head and said, "I
am certain that something has happened to one of my sons." Several
people witnessed the experience as it occurred, and the bishop wrote
down his feelings and fears about "some evil" happening to his son

later that day. It was later discovered that at that very moment, his eldest son Herbert's foot was badly crushed in an accident at sea.[1]

Fortunately, the accident wasn't fatal. This is a fairly typical example of someone sending a telepathic message to a close friend or family member while in a moment of crisis or pain.

As a child, I used to stare at the back of the head of the boy sitting at the desk in front of me and will him to turn around. Invariably, within a minute or two, he would turn around with a puzzled expression on his face and look at me. Once I'd succeeded with him, I'd focus on someone else, and I would continue doing it until the lesson came to an end. I've met several people over the years who used to do the same thing during dull classes. You may be one of them.

I wasn't aware that adults also amused themselves in a similar fashion until I read what J. B. Priestley (1894–1984), the English novelist, did at a boring poetry society dinner he attended in New York. He told the person sitting next to him, "I propose to make one of those poets wink at me." He chose a serious-looking lady for the experiment. After concentrating for a minute or two, she suddenly turned around and winked at him. Later that evening, she apologized, saying, "It was just a silly sudden impulse." [2]

You can try this simple telepathic experiment anywhere you happen to be, as long as other people are present. Choose someone who is facing away from you, stare at him or her, and mentally will the person to turn around, touch his or her ear, or do some other simple action. If you're doing this in a place where people are relaxed and comfortable, it will probably take quite a few minutes for the person to react. However, in places where people feel less safe, such as a railway station or a dark street, you'll find the person will react much more quickly. People who are naturally nervous will respond more quickly than people who are confident and feel in control of every type of situation.

---

1. Arthur Rawson Ashwell, *Life of the Right Reverend Samuel Wilberforce, Volume 1* (London: John Murray, 1880), 397.

2. J. B. Priestley, *Outcries and Asides* (London: William Heinemann Limited, 1974), 22.

You can also do this experiment in reverse. If you happen to be in a public place and sense that someone is looking at you, turn around as quickly as you can to see if someone is staring at you.

You read people's minds all the time. You may not know that you are doing it, but you frequently know what other people are thinking without a word being spoken. You're constantly receiving emotional and mental telepathic messages from others. You're also sensing people's thoughts and feelings from their body language and facial expressions.

I'm sure you can tell if someone is happy, angry, tense, or sad with just a casual glance. You can tell if someone is nervous but is trying to conceal the fact. If you walk into a room shortly after two people have had an argument, you can feel the atmosphere, even if the people concerned are trying to act as if everything is going well.

Recently, after I gave a presentation to a large company, I went to thank the lady who had booked me. A man left her office as I arrived, and I walked straight in. The lady appeared bright and cheerful, but it was obvious the discussion she'd had moments earlier had not been a pleasant one. She immediately opened the box of chocolates I gave her and visibly relaxed as she put one in her mouth. Although nothing was said about the earlier conversation, the tension in the air was obvious despite her attempts to behave normally.

As well as receiving thoughts and emotions from others, you are subconsciously sending out your thoughts and emotions. If, for instance, you dislike someone at work, you'll unknowingly telepathically transmit those feelings to the other person. As there's likely to be emotion attached to those thoughts, the other person cannot fail to receive them. If you're extremely fond of someone, you'll subconsciously send out thoughts of love, which will be picked up by the object of your affection. These are examples of the old saying "where your thoughts go, energy flows." It really does pay to be careful what you think about.

Have you ever had the experience of knowing what someone is going to say before they've said a single word? Alternatively, you might have said exactly what the person you happened to be with was thinking. Maybe you and a friend started to say the same thing simultaneously. Experiences of this sort commonly occur between people in close relationships, but they can also occur between casual acquaintances and work colleagues. Obviously, in cases of this sort, you may simply happen to have the same thoughts at the same time. However, this is such a common experience that, at least some of the time, you will be reading each other's minds.

Because of all of this, I'm confident you have the ability to know what other people are thinking. You can send and receive thoughts. However, if you're like most people, it happens randomly. The thought may also be so quiet and gentle that sometimes you fail to pick it up.

You have already experienced numerous examples of mind reading. Have you ever phoned someone and found the line was engaged as they were trying to call you at the exact same time? Have you ever thought of someone you haven't seen for a long time and then immediately received a phone call, e-mail, or letter from them? Examples such as these occur so regularly that chances are we don't even comment on them.

In addition to experiences of this sort, you also read minds in virtually every communication you have with others. You use your powers of observation, along with memories, emotions, and reason, to work out what the other person is thinking about. This ability enables you to understand others and get along well with them. People who have difficulty in doing this experience major problems in functioning effectively in society.

Women are usually expected to be better than men at sending and receiving thoughts. This could be because of the incredible psychic bond that develops between a mother and a child, or possibly because women are generally considered to be more open to psychic influences than men. However, anyone can learn how to do it. At a conference at the Institute of Noetic Sciences in 2003, 465 people were asked a series of questions about different aspects of their lives, including psychic experiences. The results found that 85 percent of the people with telepathic abilities were female.[3]

Some people are naturally better at sending messages; others are better at receiving them. However, with practice, it's possible to learn how to do both.

It's easier to pick up strong, emotional feelings than it is to pick up an idle thought about nothing in particular. Major disasters and emergencies produce enormous power, and that's why it's easier for other people to pick up on these thoughts.

The purpose of this book is to help you to consciously send and receive thoughts. It will give you a hidden edge in all your dealings with others. For instance, you'll be able to silently influence others with your thoughts. You'll be able to pick up other people's silent messages. This ability will enhance your communication skills and enable you to perceive more than you ever thought possible.

In chapter 1, you'll discover that you are already a mind reader, as the chances are you regularly pick up thoughts from family and friends. You also send thoughts to them in return.

In chapter 2, you'll look at one way of classifying people. You'll learn how to recognize different personality types and use that information to determine how people process their thoughts and emotions. You'll also discover how your beliefs and assumptions affect your ability to send and receive thoughts.

Chapter 3 covers the important topic of gaining rapport with others, and it teaches you how to feel and sense other people's energy. You'll also discover your dominant sense and learn the power of reading people's eye movements as you converse with them.

---

3. Sophy Burnham, *The Art of Intuition: Cultivating Your Inner Wisdom* (New York: Jeremy P. Tarcher / Penguin, 2011).

Chapter 4 teaches you how to read people's thoughts by observing their body language. In fact, many people will believe you are reading minds once you master the basics of nonverbal communication.

In chapter 5, you'll start experimenting with mind-to-mind communication. This chapter discusses the necessary preparation, state of mind, and some initial "warm-up" experiments to help you develop your mind-reading skills as quickly as possible.

Chapter 6 discusses experiments in mind reading that you can do over the phone and by e-mail. It also teaches you how to contact someone telepathically and ask him or her to contact you.

Chapter 7 involves mind-reading experiments using playing cards, ESP cards, and other types of cards. Some of these experiments replicate those done in research laboratories around the world.

Chapter 8 looks at some more-advanced experiments using photographs, drawings, dice, and even jokes. The famous ganzfeld experiments are discussed, and instructions are given to enable you to experience the ganzfeld yourself. Finally, the Japanese art of haragei, or belly talk, is discussed. If you've ever had a "gut feeling" about something, you'll enjoy the two experiments using haragei.

Chapter 9 teaches you the fascinating art of contact mind reading, and it includes a variety of experiments to demonstrate this skill. With the information in this chapter, you'll be able to entertain, as well as educate, your friends and family.

Chapter 10 contains a number of group tests that you can experiment with whenever you are with a group of like-minded people.

Many, if not most, pet owners believe they can communicate telepathically with their pet. Chapter 11 contains a number of experiments you can do with your pet.

Chapter 12 discusses dreams. Many people have experienced telepathic and precognitive dreams. This chapter discusses telepathic dreams, lucid dreaming, and interspecies telepathic dreaming.

Chapter 13 looks at ways in which your mind-reading skills can be used to enhance psychic readings. You do not need to be a psychic reader to benefit from these, as you can also use them yourself to find answers to problems and concerns in your own life.

Chapter 14 discusses various ways you can use your mind-reading skills in everyday life.

If you're like me, you'll be tempted to start by reading the chapters that appear most interesting to you. There's nothing wrong with that, but you'll learn more quickly if you read this book from start to finish first and then return to the chapters that interest you the most.

There are two ways to work with the experiments. You might like to try all of the experiments chapter by chapter as you read them. Alternatively, you might prefer to read the entire book, and then start on the experiments.

Let's move on to chapter 1, where you'll discover that you are already a mind reader.

There's nothing to this telepathy business. It's all in the mind.
—ROBERT BLOCH

chapter 1

YOU ARE ALREADY
A MIND READER

Frederic Myers (1843–1901), a well-known psychic researcher and one of the founders of the Society for Psychical Research, coined the word *telepathy* in 1882. He created the word to describe "the communication of impressions of any kind from one mind to another independently of the recognized channels of sense."[4] The word *telepathy* is derived from two Greek words: *tele*, which means "distant," and *pathe*, which means "feeling." Someone who can send and receive thoughts, feelings, and emotions is called a telepath.

There are two types of mind reading. The first is spontaneous, and it usually occurs at a time of crisis. An example of this would be when someone in distress sends out a call for help to a close friend or loved one. The second is a deliberate act that is usually organized and premeditated. It is this second type of mind reading that we'll be concerned with in this book.

Scientific investigation into telepathy began in the 1880s, when the Society for Psychical Research and the American Society for Psychical

---

4. F. W. H. Myers, *Proceedings of the Society for Psychical Research 1*, 2 (1882): 147.

Research were formed. These were influential organizations in their time, and many eminent people belonged to them. Lord Tennyson, Mark Twain, Sigmund Freud, Aldous Huxley, and William Gladstone were all members. Initially, the Society for Psychical Research established six committees to look at different areas of the psychic world. One of these was thought transference, the ability to transfer information from one mind to another. The word *telepathy*, which is the word we use for thought transference today, was coined later in the same year (1882). Their first experiments consisted of someone transmitting a number, image, or taste to someone in another room. This marked the start of serious research into mind reading.

Numerous theories have been put forward to explain telepathy, but so far none have been able to be proven scientifically. In medieval times, writers suggested that telepathy was a "sense of nature" that enabled one person to experience the feelings of others. In the nineteenth century, Sir William Crookes (1832–1919), the British chemist, physicist, and psychic researcher, thought that telepathy used brain waves. Leonid L. Vasiliev (1891–1966), the Russian parapsychologist, believed thoughts were conducted by electromagnetic radiation. Jan Ehrenwald (1900–1988), the Czechoslovakian psychiatrist and psychotherapist, postulated that telepathy came into being to bridge the communication gap between mothers and babies who could not yet speak. Lawrence LeShan, the American psychologist and educator, suggested that quantum mechanics and the quantum theory helped explain telepathy and clairvoyance. Many people believe that telepathy has a spiritual basis and uses our higher consciousness to send and receive telepathic messages.

Telepathy Between Family Members

Telepathy usually occurs when there is a strong emotional link between the two people involved. Consequently, there are probably more reports of telepathy between family members than any other types of mind reading.

Twins, especially identical twins, are believed to have a special psychic connection with each other. The now eighty-year-old identical twins from Scotland, Fay Hunter and Joy Dundas, are a good example. In 1962, a Scottish newspaper reported how they sent each other identical birthday cards. Fay now lives in New Zealand, and Joy lives in Australia. In 2014, they again sent each other the same card for their birthday. Their brother, still living in Scotland, used to receive identical birthday cards from his sisters almost every year. Eventually, he complained about this, and the sisters now check first to make sure they send him different cards. Fay's husband says, "It's uncanny at times. I think it's a form of telepathy."[5]

In 1961, Dr. J. B. Rhine (1895–1980), the father of modern parapsychology, encouraged Olivia Rivers, a psychologist at Mississippi State University, to investigate two identical twelve-year-old twins, Terry and Sherry Young. These young girls were able to communicate telepathically with each other in complete sentences. Even when they were put into different classrooms, much to the frustration of their teachers, they wrote similar sentences and received identical marks.[6]

There are many recorded instances of people suddenly "knowing" when someone close to them was in danger. Here is a well-documented example that involved a father and his daughter.

On October 5, 1965, William Freed woke up in Wellington, New Zealand, "with a strong feeling that something was wrong with my younger daughter, Anna." There was no obvious reason for his concern. When he had last heard from her, she was enjoying a wonderful vacation in the Balearic Islands. However, his feeling of unease was

---

5. Jon Andrews, "'Telepathic' Twins Share a Special 80th Birthday," *Bayside Leader*, Cheltenham, Australia (Feb. 25, 2014): 3, http://leader.newspaperdirect.com /epaper/viewer.aspx.

6. "Telepathy Ability Is Reportedly Displayed in Twin Sisters, 12," *The San Bernardino County Sun*, October 11, 1961, http://www.newspapers.com/newspage/53974197/.

so strong that he tried to contact his wife who was on vacation in Europe. He phoned a mutual friend in London with no success. He then called a friend in Paris, who told him his wife had been in Paris and was on her way to London. He called the friend in London two more times, each time with no success. Finally, he called his elder daughter, who lived in Brisbane, Australia. As international phone calls were extremely expensive in the 1960s she was surprised to receive a call from her father, especially as it concerned a mere feeling. She was unable to help either.

That evening, Mr. Freed received a phone call from his wife in London. She had heard that Anna was seriously ill in Formentera, in the Balearic Islands, and she needed him to contact the New Zealand External Affairs Department to arrange a flight for her to go to Majorca, where she would be met by the British consul. When Mrs. Freed finally reached the Balearic Islands, she found that Anna was feeling much better, and a few days later she was able to travel with her back to London. However, for several days—the period that Mr. Freed was concerned about her, even though he was twelve thousand miles away—she had been seriously ill.[7]

This is an excellent example of mind-to-mind communication, as all the phone calls and dealings with hospitals and authorities could be verified. How did Mr. Freed receive these thoughts from a daughter who, as far as he knew, was enjoying a wonderful vacation?

While I was writing this chapter I visited a supermarket to buy a few items. I'd accidentally left my cell phone at home, and my wife, Margaret, couldn't call me to say she wanted me to buy some raw sugar. When I arrived home, she started to tell me the story, and I amazed her, and myself, by producing the sugar she wanted. Without realizing it, I'd picked up her thought and bought the sugar along with the other items. I didn't consciously pick up a thought saying, "Buy raw sugar," but I somehow added it to my mental list and bought it

---

7. *Journal of the British Society for Psychical Research* (March 1968): 237–239.

without even consciously querying whether or not we needed sugar. I don't recall ever buying raw sugar before. Obviously, I simply picked up Margaret's thoughts and acted on them. You may have had a similar experience.

Telepathy and Empathy

Empathy is the ability to imagine yourself in someone else's shoes and understand that person's thoughts, feelings, and actions. The word *empathy* was coined in 1909 by Edward Titchener (1867–1927), an American psychologist.[8] The word is derived from the Greek word *pathos*, which means "emotion, feeling, compassion, and suffering." It's also related to the German word *Einfühlung*, which means "sympathy."

We all pick up other people's feelings and emotions. We do this automatically all the time, and we usually think nothing of it. Because empathy is such a fundamental part of human nature, we're all unconsciously using our telepathic abilities every day without realizing it.

This means that whenever you mentally place yourself in someone else's shoes, you're experiencing what it must be like to be him or her at that moment. Consequently, you're effectively reading that person's mind.

Every social interaction contains at least some element of telepathy. Thinking positive thoughts toward the other person increases harmony and rapport and makes the encounter more enjoyable for both people. Conversely, thinking negative thoughts limits the potential and pleasure of the interaction. The same thing applies in groups as well as one-on-one conversations. This is why the attitude of the CEO is so important for all companies, as his or her attitudes and feelings subliminally affect every member of the staff. The average CEO would probably laugh if told that the success of his or her corporation

---

8. Karsten Stueber, "Empathy," *The Stanford Encyclopedia of Philosophy* (Spring 2014 Edition), Edward N. Zalta (ed.), http://plato.stanford.edu/archives/spr2014/entries/empathy/.

depended partly on the telepathic messages he or she was sending out to everyone on the payroll and that every one of those people was capable of sending and receiving telepathic messages. We are all capable of being good mind readers.

In the next chapter, we'll see how people's different personality types help us read thoughts and emotions.

The more you like yourself, the less you are like anyone else,
which makes you unique.

—WALT DISNEY

chapter 2

EVERYONE IS DIFFERENT

Whenever you meet someone for the first time, you gain an immediate impression of his or her personality. You do this unconsciously. Most of the time, your subconscious assessment of the person will be correct. This is why you can be instantly attracted to someone and immediately distrust someone else. For everyday purposes, this remarkable ability is enough. However, there are occasions when it can be useful to systematically evaluate someone's personality. If you're thinking about employing someone, for instance, you'll want as much information as possible about the person's intelligence, honesty, skills, and ability at getting along with others.

Fortunately, over the years many different systems have been created to help people understand their own, as well as other people's, personalities. Once you've gained insight into someone's personality, you'll find it easier to read his or her mind. This is because you'll understand how the person thinks, and you'll also know the role emotions play in his or her life.

In the 1930s, Gordon Allport (1897–1967), a professor of psychology at Harvard University, started examining people's traits as part of his work in the new field of personality psychology. He began by going through *Webster's New International Dictionary*, writing down every word he could find that described a person.

After reducing the initial total of 17,953 entries, he arrived at 4,500 traits.[9] He split these up into three groups that he called cardinal, central, and secondary. The cardinal traits were the driving traits that shape a person's character, such as a need for fame. The central traits were basic traits, such as punctuality and honesty. The secondary traits were traits that are apparent only in certain situations. These include the person's attitudes and preferences. If someone was terrified of public speaking, for example, his or her anxiety about this would only appear when he or she had to stand up and speak.

Other psychologists continued to refine Dr. Allport's study. By the early 1980s, the list had been reduced to just five words, a grouping that Lewis Goldberg, Professor Emeritus at the University of Oregon, termed the "Big Five."[10] They are conscientiousness, agreeableness, neuroticism, openness, and extroversion. Everyone contains a degree of each of these traits. It is the unique combination of these traits that creates a person's personality.

Conscientiousness

People who rate well in conscientiousness are hard-working, responsible, reliable, thoughtful, goal-oriented, and possess good self-control. They are well-organized and prefer working toward long-term

---

9. G. W. Allport and H. S. Odbert, "Trait Names: A Psycholexical Study," *Psychological Monographs* 47 (1936): Whole No. 211.

10. Lewis R. Goldberg and Tina K. Rosolack, "The Big Five Factor Structure as an Integrative Framework: An Empirical Comparison with Eysenck's P-E-N Model," in *The Developing Structure of Temperament and Personality from Infancy to Adulthood*, eds. C. F. Halverson Jr., G. A. Kohnstamn, and R. P. Martin (New York: Erlbaum, 1994), 7–35.

goals rather than short-term ones. They love details and prefer to plan ahead, rather than act spontaneously.

People who rate low in conscientiousness are disorganized, unreliable, and become discouraged quickly.

Agreeableness

People who rate well in agreeableness are cooperative, compassionate, considerate, modest, good-natured, caring, kind, helpful, and willing to make adjustments to fit in. They are trusting and tend to see the best in other people. They pay attention to other people's needs and like to get on with others.

People who rate low in agreeableness are unfriendly, aloof, and make no effort to get along with others. They tend to compete, rather than cooperate, with others.

Neuroticism

People who rate high in neuroticism are anxious, self-conscious, suspicious, and insecure. They experience negative emotions, such as anger, depression, and vulnerability, more readily than other people. They get upset easily, tend to hold grudges, and are prone to stress.

People who rate low in neuroticism are stable, secure, calm, and handle stress easily. (This is why some books call this category "emotional stability," and use neuroticism as the negative aspect. I've retained neuroticism, as that is the form in which the Big Five began, and most books still reflect this.)

Openness

People who rate well in openness are imaginative nonconformists who enjoy coming up with good ideas. They tend to be intellectual, imaginative, and creative. They are naturally curious and enjoy new experiences and opportunities to experience fresh and different activities. They tend to be independent in thought and action.

People who rate low in openness are intolerant, disinterested, and become bored easily.

Extroversion

People who rate well in extroversion are outgoing, enthusiastic, energetic lovers of excitement and stimulation. They enjoy being the center of attention. They are positive, sociable, talkative, and assertive. They thrive in company and enjoy meeting new people.

People who rate low in extroversion are shy, timid, and nervous.

You can test your ratings in each of these attributes online, at www.outofservice.com/bigfive/.

Once you've determined which category someone belongs in, you'll know how they'll think in any given situation. For instance, when two people meet each other for the first time at a cocktail party, they'll start by exchanging pleasantries while looking for clues about each other.

The predominantly conscientious person will be thoughtful and considerate. He or she is likely to have arrived at the party right on time.

The predominantly agreeable person will be sociable, easy to get along with, and interested in other people. He or she will work hard to ensure other people feel relaxed and at ease.

The predominately neurotic person will wonder if the other person likes him or her and will be concerned about the impression he or she is making. He or she is likely to feel nervous and may have felt anxious in the days leading up to the event.

The predominantly open person will be able to discuss almost anything, and he or she will bring a new, imaginative perspective to the conversation.

The predominantly extrovert person will be excitable and talkative and will enjoy being the center of attention. He or she will talk to many people, smile and laugh frequently, and will have no difficulty starting conversations.

Although recognizing the character traits of the Big Five doesn't tell you what someone is thinking, it will provide valuable clues about his or her personality. Knowing this enables you to know what a person would be likely to think, say, and do in any given situation. Of course, this isn't foolproof, as everyone acts out of character occasionally. As this is hard, not to mention stressful, to do, few people manage to stay out of character for long. Consequently, most of the time, the Big Five will provide you with valuable clues about what other people are likely to be thinking about, and this means you're starting to read people's minds.

Beliefs and Assumptions

We all have a large number of false assumptions and beliefs that influence our lives in many different ways. Everything we see, hear, or do is affected by the beliefs that are hidden in our subconscious minds. It's wonderful when these are positive beliefs, but unfortunately, they're more likely to be negative beliefs and assumptions that constrict and stifle our potential. The sad thing is that many of these were implanted in us in early childhood, and they were accepted by us when we were children and believed everything authority figures, such as teachers and parents, told us.

Fortunately, we also have good assumptions and beliefs that help us make sense of the world we live in. All of them, good and bad, have become habits as a result of years of repetition.

When I was a child at school, my French teacher told me that I was hopeless at learning languages. I believed him, and for thirty years I didn't even try to learn a foreign language, as, after all, I knew I was "hopeless" at it.

More than twenty years ago, I attended the Frankfurt Book Fair. I had very little money, and I stayed in a small town many miles away because I couldn't afford to stay in Frankfurt itself. One morning, I caught the wrong train by mistake. It was a Regional Express rather than the local train I was supposed to be on. Despite the intervention of a few people on the train who spoke on my behalf, the ticket inspector gave me an instant fine. This consumed most of my food budget, so for the rest of my time in Frankfurt I ate virtually nothing except breakfast, which was included in the hotel booking. I returned to New Zealand determined to learn enough German to be able to avoid accidentally catching the wrong trains and to be able to talk to the ticket inspector if I ever made the same mistake again.

To my surprise, I found it comparatively easy to learn German. I've returned to the Frankfurt Book Fair many times since then, and my enjoyment of it has increased enormously because I've been able to speak with the locals in their language. I'm definitely not hopeless at learning languages, yet for a large part of my life I believed I was.

When my mother was very young, someone a year or two older than her told her she couldn't sing. For the rest of her life she never sang in public, as she "knew" she couldn't sing. The only place she ever sang was at home when she was doing household chores. In actuality, she had a pleasant voice and was able to sing in tune. She deprived herself of a great deal of pleasure because she believed something that definitely wasn't true.

Everyone has different beliefs and assumptions. When you send a thought to someone, it will originate in your mind and be filtered and altered by your personal assumptions and beliefs. The person receiving your thought will filter it through his or her assumptions and beliefs and try to make sense of your message.

Obviously, many messages will be misunderstood or misconstrued, as everyone is different and looks at life in his or her own unique way. Consequently, before telepathically transmitting a message to someone you need to make an effort to see the world through his or her eyes. If you consciously do this, you'll be able to bypass their assumptions and beliefs and send and receive clear thoughts.

Of course, if you believe that mind reading is an impossibility, that will become your reality, and you'll find it difficult to read minds until you've changed your belief.

It's impossible to make a close telepathic connection with anyone without first gaining rapport. In the next chapter, we'll explore a variety of effective ways to gain rapport with others.

The most important single ingredient in the formula of success
is knowing how to get along with people.
—THEODORE ROOSEVELT

chapter 3

GETTING ON WITH OTHERS

It's much easier to read people's minds when you're in rapport with them. Dictionaries define *rapport* as a harmonious, empathetic, or compassionate connection between two or more people. You create rapport automatically when you're with friends and people you like. This is why you can often know what a friend is thinking, but you find it harder to pick up the thoughts of strangers. Fortunately, there are a number of techniques you can use to gain rapport with others, and this will make it easier for you to read their minds. You'll also find it will make you more effective in all of your interactions with others.

Mind-Reading Rapport

In the introduction, I mentioned that I used to will people in my classes at school to turn around. This is a simple mind-reading exercise that anyone can do. There's another experiment that you've probably done throughout your life without knowing it. You do this by sending out thoughts of friendship whenever you meet someone. If you approach everyone with thoughts of cordiality, friendship, harmony, and cooperation, you'll find that most of the time the other person will receive these thoughts from you and respond in a similar way in return.

You might even say to yourself before meeting someone: "This is going to be a good relationship. We're going to be friends." Of course, by thinking these thoughts, you'll also act accordingly, and your friendliness and positivity will be visible in your face, body, actions, tone of voice, and words.

This works for groups as well as individuals. I worked in the entertainment industry for many years, and I know many entertainers who always tell themselves they love their audiences before walking on stage. The audience picks up on these thoughts and acts accordingly.

The Power of Focus

One of the easiest ways to gain rapport is to focus entirely on the other person. Forget about yourself and do everything you can to make the other person feel comfortable and relaxed.

Recently I've been mentoring a young magician who suffered terribly from stage fright. Before every performance he'd worry that the audience wouldn't like him, that he wouldn't make a good impression, and that he'd mess up a trick. He was putting all of the emphasis on himself rather than on the people he was being paid to entertain. Once he started focusing on how to make the experience as enjoyable as possible for the audience, he became more entertaining and much more successful. As a bonus, his stage fright disappeared.

There are a number of techniques that can be used to help you gain rapport. The first is to match the other person's mood. No matter what mood you happen to be in, you'll always enjoy spending time with someone in a similar state of mind. The saying "misery loves company" is true. Miserable people like other miserable people. Happy people associate with happy people. Enthusiastic people love people who are also enthusiastic. People like people who are similar to them.

It's easier to gain rapport with someone if you match his or her mood. If you're naturally gregarious and outgoing and want to gain rapport with someone who's quiet and shy, you'll have to tone down your energy until you've gained rapport. Similarly, if you're the quiet person, you'll need to make an effort to raise your energy to gain rapport with the other person.

It may sound contrived to deliberately match someone's mood. However, you do this automatically whenever you spend time with your friends. If you visit a friend who is feeling full of the joys of life, you'll match his or her mood without even knowing you're doing it. Conversely, if your friend is feeling sad and subdued, you'll automatically lower your energy levels. Once you've attained rapport with someone, you can gradually return to your normal self and chances are the other person will follow your lead.

Mirroring

Mirroring is the term used when two people imitate each other's body language and movements. In the same way that you match other people's energy levels, mirroring is also done unconsciously when you're with someone you like. You can test this next time you spend time with a friend. At some stage during the conversation, pause to see how you're positioned, and then look at your friend. Chances are you'll both be exhibiting similar postures. If you or your friend has a hand resting on the table, for instance, the other person will probably be doing the same.

When you consciously mirror someone's posture, you need to do it carefully, sensitively, and with respect. Mimicking the other person can cause offense, as it looks as if you're making fun of the other person's posture.

Mirroring

Once you've become familiar with how two people who are in rapport unconsciously mirror each other's body language, you'll be able to look at larger groups and see which people are in rapport and which are not. I enjoy doing this at my local coffee shop. It's easy to see which people are friends, which couples don't get on, who is being interviewed by someone else, and so on.

You can also experiment by deliberately mismatching your posture to that of the other person. You'll find the flow of conversation and how the other person reacts to you will change. Once you start mirroring the other person again, you'll find that you'll both become more relaxed and the conversation will flow freely once more.

When I first learned about mirroring, I tried to do it with everyone I spoke with. However, I quickly discovered that this wasn't possible with people who fidget, as they constantly change their posture. Any attempt to mirror them would be noticed right away, creating the opposite effect to the one intended. Fortunately, there is something you can do when you find yourself with someone who is fidgeting. This technique is called cross matching.

To cross match, match one part of the other person's body with a different part of your body. If the other person is sitting with his or her legs crossed, for instance, you might cross your arms. If the person has his or her legs open, you might hold your hands well apart. If the person is tapping his or her fingers, you might tap a foot or very slightly move your head as if following the rhythm of a song.

Cross matching

Once you've mirrored the other person, you can do a test to see if you've gained rapport. Wait two or three minutes, and then change your posture slightly. If you're in rapport, the other person will also change his or her posture. This won't happen immediately. It might happen within seconds, but could take as long as two minutes. The person's change of posture may not exactly mirror what you did, but it tells you that he or she is subconsciously following your lead and is in rapport with you.

You need do this only once. You risk losing rapport if you continue to test throughout the conversation. However, you should do it again if you're reestablishing rapport after an interruption, such as a phone call or someone coming in to speak to you about a completely different matter.

Synchronized Breathing

Matching your rate of breathing with the other person is another powerful way to increase rapport. This is undetectable by the other person, but it increases rapport at a subconscious level. You can use it on its own or increase overall rapport by using it in combination with mirroring. The easiest way to do this is to observe the shoulders or chest of the other person, and then match your breathing with the other person's inhalations and exhalations.

This can be a useful way to gain rapport with someone you're speaking to on the telephone. You can't match his or her posture, as you don't know what it is, but you can hear the other person's breathing.

Visual, Auditory, or Kinesthetic

Our reality is based on what we see, hear, and feel. Our senses of taste and smell are also included in this, but their influence is minor compared to the others. We make use of all of these senses, but in most people one of the senses is dominant.

Someone who experiences life primarily through images is called a visual person. Likewise, someone who experiences life primarily through the sense of sound is known as an auditory person. Someone who perceives life primarily through touching and feeling is called a kinesthetic person. (Kinesthetic comes from the ancient Greek words *cine*, which means "put in motion," and *aesthesis*, which means "sensation.")

Everyone, no matter what his or her primary sense is, makes use of the other senses. Someone who is primarily auditory, for instance, also makes use of his or her eyes and feelings. However, this person will depend on hearing more than, say, his or her sense of vision.

The Visual Person

About 60 percent of the world's population is visual. This demonstrates just how powerful our sense of sight is. Visual people enjoy watching and examining. They are good at remembering what they read. When spelling a difficult word they'll "see" it in their mind. Visual people speak quickly and use plenty of gestures to get their points across.

As we all use language that is intimately connected with our thoughts, visual people use phrases such as: "I can see what you're saying," "That's clear," "I can picture that," "We see eye to eye," "Let's keep this in perspective," "Let's focus on this," and "Do you see my point?"

The Auditory Person

About 30 percent of the population are primarily auditory people. Auditory people love pleasing sounds, but they are affected more than most people by harsh sounds, such as loud sirens. They like talking and can easily take over a conversation. However, they also enjoy listening and are good at remembering what people have said. They are sensitive to another's tone of voice, and they can be easily hurt when reprimanded or criticized if the other person's tone of voice is perceived to be harsh. They enjoy humming and talking to themselves.

They don't like to be rushed and prefer to process information carefully before acting.

They tend to use phrases such as: "That's as clear as a bell," "Something went *click* in my mind," "Something tells me," "That's loud and clear," "Hear me out," "That rings true to me," and "How does that sound to you?"

The Kinesthetic Person

Approximately 10 percent of the population is primarily kinesthetic. Kinesthetic people live in a world of feelings. No one can express the joys of love and happiness better than a kinesthetic person. They also have a heightened sense of touch, which makes them highly capable at anything that involves a hands-on approach. This response to touch means they enjoy receiving handshakes, hugs, pats on the back, arms around their shoulders, and touches on the arm. They enjoy movement and often walk around while performing a task. Kinesthetic people act on their feelings and frequently make decisions based on their emotions.

They tend to use phrases such as: "I have a gut feeling about this," "I sense you could be right," "I'll be in touch with you," "I can't get a grip on that," "There's no need to get pushy," "I'll handle this," or "How do you feel about that?"

Once you recognize someone's dominant sense, you can gain rapport by speaking in terms that resonate well with them. If, for instance, you said, "I see" in reply to something said by a visual person, you'd be well on your way to gaining rapport with him.

Here's a conversation between two people with different dominant senses.

JOHN: Wow! You're as pretty as a picture tonight.
KAREN: I don't feel that well.
JOHN: But you look great.

KAREN: I'm a bit tense and stressed. I feel a cold coming on.

JOHN: Well, I see we'll have to change our plans for tonight.

John is obviously visual and Karen is kinesthetic. This conversation is likely to prove annoying for both of them, as they're effectively speaking different languages. Here's what the conversation might sound like if John paid attention to Karen's preferred representational system.

JOHN: Wow! You're as pretty as a picture tonight.

KAREN: I don't feel that well.

JOHN: Here, give me a cuddle. You need a bit of hands-on attention.

KAREN: I'm a bit tense and stressed. I feel a cold coming on.

JOHN: You poor thing. Let me hold you close. Rather than go out, maybe we should stay here, and I can look after you. How do you feel about that?

By speaking to Karen using her preferred way of expressing herself, John has gained the rapport he desired.

Am I Visual, Auditory, or Kinesthetic?

This questionnaire will enable you to find out which is your dominant sense. You'll find that you, like everyone else, use all three, but one will be more dominant than the others.

1. When learning how to operate a new electronic device, do you:
   a. Read the instructions
   b. Ask someone to explain it all to you
   c. Try it out and learn by "trial and error"

2. When meeting an old friend, do you say:
   a. "It's great to see you!"
   b. "How wonderful to hear your voice!"
   c. "Give me a hug!"

3. When you're shopping, do you:
   a. Look at different items and then decide which one to buy
   b. Ask the staff in the shop for help and advice
   c. Handle the object, test it, and if it's an item of clothing, try it on

4. When you're angry, do you:
   a. Constantly replay in your mind what it was that made you angry
   b. Shout, scream, and tell everyone all about what happened
   c. Stomp your way through the house or office, slamming doors and hitting things

5. When you write a word that is difficult to spell, do you:
   a. Look at the word in your mind's eye to see if it looks right
   b. Say the word out loud or hear it in your mind
   c. Sense or feel that the word is spelled correctly

6. When you make a decision, do you:
   a. Picture all the possible choices in your mind
   b. Hear both sides of a conversation in your mind
   c. Gain a sense of how you'd feel if each possible choice came into being

7. When you're relaxing, would you like to:
   a. Watch television or go to the movies
   b. Read a book or listen to music
   c. Do something physical, such as gardening, home maintenance, or playing a sport

8. When walking around an unfamiliar city, do you:
   a. Carry a map you can refer to
   b. Ask people for directions
   c. Follow your instincts

9. When listening to a song, do you:
    a. Sing the lyrics, either silently or aloud
    b. Listen to the lyrics and the music
    c. Move in time to the music

10. When you're anxious about something, do you:
    a. Visualize all the things that could go wrong
    b. Talk to yourself about the problem
    c. Fidget, move around, tap your fingers and feet, and find it hard to stay still

11. What do you remember most from your last visit to a beach?
    a. How beautiful the setting was—the sun, the blue of the sea, and the whiteness of the sand
    b. The sounds made by the waves, birds, people, and the breeze
    c. The feeling of the sand beneath your feet, the coolness of the water, and the breeze on your face

12. When given an assignment at work, do you prefer:
    a. To have a clear picture of what's required in your mind
    b. Someone to tell you what is required
    c. To have a sense or feeling of what is required

13. One of your strong points is your ability to:
    a. See what is going on
    b. Hear what sounds right
    c. Be aware of your feelings and be able to act on them

14. When speaking with people, are you likely to say:
    a. "I see where you're coming from"
    b. "I hear you loud and clear"
    c. "That feels right to me"

15. When you're in rapport with someone, you:
    a. See him or her in an easy-to-get-along-with, highly enjoyable, way
    b. Hear him or her expressing views in exactly the same way that you would
    c. Sense that the other person feels about you in the exact same way you feel about him or her

Count the number of a's, b's, and c's to see which one is your dominant sense. The a's indicate visual, b's auditory, and the c's kinesthetic.

As we all make use of all three of these, the result may not always be clear. It's obvious someone is visual if he gets, for instance, nine visual, four auditory, and two kinesthetic. It's not nearly as clear if someone gets five visual, five auditory, and five kinesthetic. If that occurs, the best thing is to wait a couple of days and do the test again. If the result is still the same, it shows you're making good use of all three modes. One is likely to be slightly dominant, but many of your strategies will make use of the other two modes.

How to Feel Other People's Energy

Have you ever walked into a room where two people have just had an argument? Although the people involved might look relaxed and happy, you probably felt the anger and tension in the room. You've probably experienced similar situations when you've spent time with people who were nervous, sick, or worried. Without a word being said, you successfully picked up the feelings and energies emanating from these people. You are bound to pick up on the vibes, or personal energies, of your friends whenever you're with them. You know when they're feeling sad, depressed, upbeat, positive, happy, or playful.

Just recently, I met someone and immediately felt a wave of grief and sadness emanating from her. I was a little bit surprised, as she was an attractive, expensively dressed, middle-aged lady with a warm and friendly smile. She looked as if she didn't have a care in the world. I learned afterward that her only child had been killed in a car accident three months earlier.

Many years ago, I worked for a husband and wife who jointly owned a business. They constantly fought and argued over everything, and you could cut the atmosphere in their office with a knife. A number of potential customers commented on the feeling in the office, even when both of them were absent. I'm sure this must have cost them a great deal of business over the years.

A few people are almost too good at sensing energies of this sort. You might think this is a good thing, but it makes life difficult for people who are overly sensitive.

"I feel nauseous whenever I'm around people who are feeling negative or sad. I pick up these feelings so easily," one lady told me. "I love being with happy people, as I pick up their feelings, too. Unfortunately, I always seem to end up working with people who express negative energy. It's hard for me to visit anyone in the hospital, as I feel their pain. I hate being in a crowd, too, as everyone's energies overwhelm me."

Most people sense other people's feelings on occasion rather than all of the time. It's a simple matter to progress from this to the stage where you can sense other people's feelings whenever you wish.

In actuality, you're sensing people and situations all of the time. You feel different at a wedding reception than you do at a business meeting or at an office party. You turn to face people and objects to sense them more deeply. You also cross your arms over your solar plexus when you feel the need for protection, as the other person's energies have been too strong. You're also sensitive to the feelings of others, especially if you're a naturally caring person.

Here's an exercise to help you develop your sensitivity.

Solo Sensitivity Exercise

Sit down comfortably and rub the palms of your hands together briskly for several seconds. Hold your hands about twelve inches apart with the palms facing each other. Slowly move your hands together. At some stage, probably when your hands are one or two inches apart, you'll feel a slight resistance, almost as if you're squashing a rubber ball between your hands. Experiment with it, pushing against it and letting it go again. Bring your hands together for a few moments, and then slowly draw them apart. You're likely to notice a sense of coolness on your palms and fingertips as you do this.

Once you've experienced this, move your hands apart, shake them briskly, and then hold them about twelve inches apart again. This time imagine that you're holding a large balloon between your hands. Press against it and sense any changes that occur in your palms. You may feel the balloon is springy, and you may sense different energies in your hands.

Finally, move to a different environment. If you've been sitting in a warm room, move to a room that has not been heated, hold your hands out and see what sensations you experience. Obviously, you'll feel changes in temperature, but you may sense other things as well. You can continue by going outdoors, into the garage, or into the attic. Try several different places and see what you can sense.

The next step is to experiment with people. You can do this anywhere you happen to be. Look at someone and see if you can sense their energy. There is nothing strange or unusual about this. It's simply a matter of paying attention and being receptive to any feelings or thoughts that come to you. You don't need to strain for information. If you remain receptive, information will flow to you. Most of this information is likely to be positive. However, there will be occasions when you feel pain, dislike, and even anger.

Sensitivity Exercise with a Partner

This is a highly enjoyable exercise that will provide stimulation and energy to both you and your partner.

Stand facing each other, three or four feet apart. Send energy to your partner. At the same time, he or she will send energy to you. This creates a current of energy that increases rapport and also provides information. As with the solo exercise, you don't need to work hard and force information to come to you. Simply focus on sending your energies out and enjoy receiving the energies being transmitted by your partner.

Once you've done this successfully, experiment by increasing the distance to several feet, a hundred yards, and ultimately a mile or more. In time, you may be able to feel your partner's energies from wherever he or she happens to be.

You can also sense groups of people. You've probably already sensed the energies put out by crowds of people immediately before sporting events, shows, and concerts. Once you're aware of it, you'll be able to do this anywhere. You can experiment by sensing people at a large department store clothing sale, while waiting in line at the supermarket or post office, and on a bus or airplane.

This knowledge will help you gain rapport with others, and it will also help keep you safe. If, for instance, you sense the mood of a crowd is turning nasty, you can leave before the situation gets out of hand.

Now that you know how to gain rapport with someone, you're well on your way to understanding how they think. In fact, you may already be doing this. In the next chapter, we'll take this a big step further and look at how facial expressions and eye cues can enable us to read minds.

You can read me baby, like an open book.

—WILL HOGE

chapter 4

I CAN READ YOU
LIKE A BOOK

Unknowingly, you, just like everyone else, communicate your
thoughts and feelings through your facial expressions and body
language. Imagine you're at a social function and happen to meet
someone. Within seconds of meeting him, you'll have made a number of decisions about him based on the way he stands, walks, holds
his head, and positions his arms and legs. All of these things reveal his
thoughts, feelings, and emotions more clearly than anything he says.

People don't usually analyze the gestures and mannerisms of others, but we pick them up unconsciously and make decisions based on
what we perceive. This is why you can instantly like or dislike someone and not know why. If asked about it later, you might say he looked
unfriendly or seemed to be too pleased with himself. However, those
judgments come later. The initial impression is gained from the person's body language.

Fortunately, it's possible to do this consciously, as well as unconsciously, and it's a particularly useful skill to learn. In fact, you already
know a great deal about the subject. If you see someone at a social

event who keeps looking downward, you'll assume that he or she is shy or may be upset about something. If you have a conversation with someone who keeps his or her arms crossed, you'll probably assume he or she is closed off and has no interest in what you're saying. If you later meet someone who maintains good eye contact, you're likely to like him or her as you'll assume he or she is interested in what you have to say. You can usually tell if someone is bored, tired, interested, or disinterested. You can recognize facial expressions, such as happiness, sadness, fear, anger, surprise, disgust, and contempt. You can tell when someone trembles with rage, shrugs his or her shoulders in indifference, taps his or her fingers in impatience, or slaps his or her forehead to indicate he or she has forgotten something.

All of this shows that you already know a great deal about body language. Even when you're not reading people's minds, people will think you are once you start paying conscious attention to the nonverbal communication of others. It's fascinating to think that you've been doing this within weeks of being born. Babies love looking at faces, and they quickly learn how to imitate people's facial expressions. At about the age of two months, babies start reacting to the emotional states of the people looking after them. Nancy Eisenberg, a professor of psychology at Arizona State University, says that at the age of twelve months "children monitor adults' expressions and use them to guide their behavior." [11] As they grow, children naturally learn to read the body language and facial expressions of their friends as they play and interact with them. They also learn these skills from the other important people in their lives, especially caregivers and teachers.

A major part of success at reading body language is observation. What would you think if someone said, "That's beautiful. I love it!" after receiving a gift and only then smiled? In this example, something is wrong with the timing. If this person was truly delighted, he or she

---

11. Nancy Eisenberg, quoted in Annie Murphy Paul, "Mind Reading," *Psychology Today*, September 2007, http://www.psychologytoday.com/articles/200708/mind-reading.

would smile while opening the gift and saying the words, rather than afterward. What would you think if someone said, "I love you," but was frowning at the same time? If you hadn't been observing what was going on, you might have missed the importance of what occurred.

These are both examples of incongruence. To be congruent, and therefore believable, our body language, tone of voice, and choice of words need to be synchronized. This is frequently referred to as the three V's: Visual, Vocal, and Verbal. This is why someone may apparently do and say all the right things, but after he or she has left, you think, *I don't trust that person.* If the person had been congruent, you probably would have trusted him or her.

You also need to pay attention to hunches and feelings. Your subconscious mind knows much more than you think. Whenever you feel unsure about a situation or a person, allow your "gut feelings" to send the necessary information to your conscious mind. You do this by simply pausing and becoming aware of your feelings. People's emotions and intentions are revealed by their body language, and you register this information subconsciously. Listening to your hunches and feelings allows your conscious mind to obtain the necessary information, which you can then act upon.

Body Language of the Face

Almost fifty years ago, Albert Mehrabian, professor emeritus of psychology at UCLA and an expert on nonverbal communication, concluded that the three important elements in face-to-face encounters were: the words, the tone of voice, and the person's body language. Words made up a mere 7 percent of the impression given, the tone of voice accounted for 38 percent, and body language was 55 percent. The body language component was 15 percent for appearance and 40 percent for facial expressions and movement. Unfortunately, his findings have been misinterpreted ever since, as they were derived solely from examining people's feelings and attitudes. However, his findings show how important the face is in person-to-person communications.

Most of the time, once you learn how to read faces, you'll know what the people you interact with are thinking.

Eyes

The eyes are the most expressive part of the face. It's no wonder they're considered "the windows to the soul." The eyes reveal the person's feelings and emotions, ranging all the way from love to hate. It's not surprising that phrases such as "if looks could kill," "look at those bedroom eyes," and "he has a roving eye" came into being.

During his lifetime, Victor Hugo (1802–1885), the famous French author of many books including *The Hunchback of Notre-Dame* and *Les Misérables*, was almost as famous for his numerous romantic relationships as he was for his writing. His memoirs are full of stories of his many sexual encounters. They also provide valuable advice on how he was so successful with women. In his memoirs he wrote: "When a woman is speaking to you, Monsieur, listen to what she has to say with her eyes." In other words, he paid attention to the feelings and expressions revealed in the eyes of the women he was wooing and reflected the messages back to them. By listening to what people have to say "with their eyes" you'll have direct access to their real thoughts and feelings, which may well be different from what they're saying.

The eyes reveal a wide range of feelings and emotions, such as trust, love, lust, hurt, anger, confusion, and impatience. When you see any of these in someone's eyes you'll know exactly what's going on in that person's mind.

Eyes Express Interest

The pupils reveal both interest and disinterest. When someone's pupils dilate, it's a sign of interest, arousal, surprise, or fear. This enables the brain to receive as much information as possible. If the pupils do the opposite and contract, the person is revealing lack of interest and indifference. It's difficult to read these signs when the lighting is bad, as everyone's pupils expand to counteract the lack of light. If the room is extremely bright, the pupils contract to counteract the extreme conditions. Consequently, before deciding if someone is interested in you, you need to check the lighting in the room to see what effect it has on the situation.

If someone is interested in you, his or her pupils will dilate. This tells you exactly what is on that person's mind.

You can test pupil dilation by looking at your eyes in front of a mirror and seeing how your pupils grow when you think of something you like.

Aristotle Onassis (1906–1975), the Greek shipping magnate, was reputed to always wear sunglasses when conducting business meetings to prevent people from reading his eyes. He also insisted that the people he was dealing with did not wear sunglasses. This gave him a huge advantage in his business negotiations.

When someone is surprised, excited, or stimulated, his or her eyes widen and the pupils dilate. This allows the brain to receive the maximum amount of information. If the surprise is positive, the eyes will stay dilated. However, if the surprise is negative, the pupils will constrict in a fraction of a second.

Like or Dislike

You can tell if someone likes you by the way he or she looks at you. Someone who likes you will look at you frequently. Someone who doesn't like you will look at you as little as possible. In both cases, you know what the other person thinks about you. Incidentally, this is not done deliberately. You naturally look at someone or something that interests you and equally as naturally look away from anything that doesn't interest you.

Eye Contact

Direct eye contact reveals interest. It also is a sign of honesty, sincerity, confidence, and open communication. If you met someone in a social situation who looked into your eyes for longer than usual, you'd probably find him or her attractive. Eye contact plays an important part in everyday conversation. It has been estimated that the speaker maintains eye contact between 40 and 60 percent of the time, and the listener maintains eye contact about 80 percent of the time.[12]

In the Western world, good eye contact is a social necessity. People who find it hard to make direct eye contact are often misunderstood. People who are shy often find it hard to make much eye contact, and some people mistakenly think these people are being deceptive or have something to hide. They may think the person has told a lie. They could think the person is feeling guilty or ashamed, for instance.

Often people who are anxious, nervous, or feel intimidated find it hard to make eye contact. They may even have come from a culture where direct eye contact is considered rude. People who have autism or Asperger's syndrome also tend to avoid making eye contact.

The degree of eye contact tells the speaker that you're paying attention to what he or she is saying. If the person's eyes start wandering, the speaker will think you're not interested in what's being said.

Someone who constantly looks over your shoulder or looks at other people while you're talking is being rude and insulting. He or she is looking for someone more important to talk to.

A direct gaze can indicate love or hate. You can read the feelings and emotions of a person who loves you in his or her eyes. Someone who is trying to intimidate you will stare at your eyes with a threatening gaze.

If you catch someone staring at you, you can tell what they're thinking from their eyes. Dilated pupils show the person likes you, but constricted pupils show the person is angry and potentially hostile.

---

12. Ken Cooper, *Nonverbal Communication for Business Success* (New York: AMACOM, 1979), 75.

Eye Expressions

The expressions made by the eyes provide valuable insights into other people's minds. If someone deliberately narrows his or her eyes, for instance, it's a sign of disapproval of something.

Glare

A glare, usually accompanied by a frown, expresses anger. This person stares at whatever is causing the irritation with wide-open, glaring eyes that silently demand that the other person change his or her behavior.

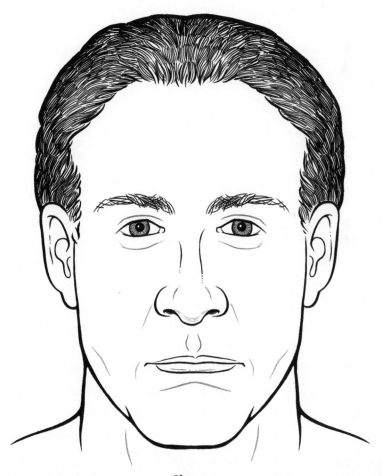

Glare

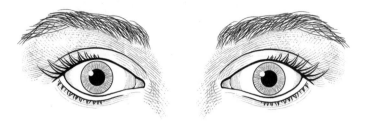

Fear

Fear

When someone is scared or afraid, his or her eyes will open wide and the eyebrows will rise and be drawn to each other. The lower eyelids will tense, and the person's lips will draw back in a straight line. The pupils dilate and the rate of blinking increases. All of this creates the "deer frozen in the headlights" expression.

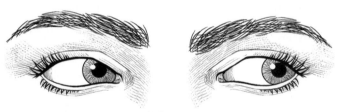

Shifty eyes

Shifty Eyes

People often move their eyes from side to side when they're feeling anxious or defensive. They may be feeling upset, disturbed, or embarrassed, or they may be insincere. It's the insincerity aspect that caused this to be known as "shifty eyes." Many people assume someone with darting eyes is lying or insincere. This could be the case, but it's more likely that he or she is feeling insecure or nervous.

Rapid eye movements from side to side indicate extreme anxiety and distress, and this shows the person desperately wants to escape a difficult situation. This situation is made even worse if the person looks downward at the same time. This is a sign of fear, disloyalty, treachery, and cowardice.

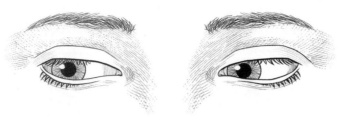

Eye dipping

Eye Dipping

Submissive people often avert their eyes downward to avoid offending someone they consider to be more dominant than them. This is a deliberate, rather than subconscious, gesture. Historically, high-status people have been free to look anywhere, but lower-status people didn't always have that right. Even today, people humble themselves by bowing their heads in the presence of royalty or someone they perceive to be of a higher status.

Looking downward is often a sign of shyness and lack of confidence. It can also be a sign of a guilty conscience.

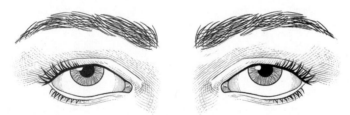

Looking upward

Looking Upward

Someone who looks upward frequently while listening to someone else is bored or unhappy with the way the conversation is progressing.

Rolling the eyes can be a sign of astonishment. However, it is usually a sign of impatience. Someone I used to work with had a habit of repeating stories over and over again. Whenever he did this, at least one person in the group would roll his or her eyes to silently say, "Here he goes again."

Looking over the top of one's spectacles

Looking over the Top of One's Spectacles

This is a sign of dominance and condescension. It can sometimes be threatening if the person dips his or her head while looking over his or her glasses. I remember a teacher from my school days who used this gesture frequently to express his disapproval of a student's behavior.

Eyes Closing

When someone is given bad news, his or her eyes will close briefly to momentarily deny the information. He or she might use a hand to block one or both eyes. If the person is holding an object, such as a newspaper or a book, he or she might use it to block the eyes.

If someone closes his or her eyes for a number of seconds, it's a sign that he or she is processing negative emotions. Sometimes the eyes will be squeezed tightly shut. This is a sign that the person is trying to block out or deny bad news.

Rubbing the Eyes

Rubbing the eyes, or blocking the eyes with a hand, are a sign that the person doesn't like what he or she is hearing. When someone is given bad news, his or her eyes will close momentarily in a subconscious attempt to deny the information. If someone touches an eye during a conversation, it's a sign that he or she isn't happy with what the other person is saying.

Blocking the Eyes

Blocking the eyes is always a negative sign. It can indicate a denial of bad news, but it also occurs when someone feels threatened, distressed, or upset. Liars sometimes block their eyes when telling a lie. (However, better liars increase, rather than reduce, their eye contact.)

Squinting

Squinting

People tend to squint when acknowledging someone they dislike or distrust. If someone doesn't like you but is forced to acknowledge you, he or she is likely to squint. The squint may be apparent for a fraction of a second, but it is easily recognizable to anyone who happens to be looking at the person at the time.

People also squint when they feel uncomfortable. If they lower their eyebrows at the same time, it's a sign of loss of confidence.

It's a sign of uncertainty if someone squints while reading a contract or any other important document. Good salespeople are alert to this, and they are ready to explain exactly what the words that are causing the problem mean.

Some people deliberately squint and lower their eyebrows to intimidate others and make sure they get their own way.

Disbelief or doubt are shown by narrowing the eyes, furrowing the brow, and raising an eyebrow. It's a sign that the person is questioning whatever is going on.

Blinking and Fluttering

In normal situations, people blink six to eight times a minute. People blink more when they feel nervous, agitated, stressed, upset, or pressured. They'll continue blinking rapidly until they feel relaxed. President Richard M. Nixon appeared calm and relaxed during most of his resignation speech. However, every now and again he blinked excessively, revealing the incredible pressure he was under. As a result of this, Joseph Tecce, professor of psychology at Boston College, calls rapid blinking in uncomfortable situations the "Nixon effect." [13]

Eyelid flutter is more serious, as it shows the person is upset about something. The fluttering continues until the person is able to release whatever it was that caused the upset from his or her mind.

At a party I hosted a few years ago, one of the guests made an ill-advised comment about gay people. Although the lady next to me didn't say anything, I noticed her eyelids began fluttering. As I wanted all my guests to feel comfortable, I immediately changed the subject, and after about ten seconds the fluttering slowed and gradually stopped. When I told my wife about this incident afterward, she told me that it was probably because someone in the woman's immediate family had recently come out as being gay.

------

13. Gordon R. Wainwright, *Master Body Language,* rev. ed. by Richard Thompson (London: Hodder Education, 2011), 6.

Eye Movements

Ralph Waldo Emerson (1803–1882) wrote, "The eye obeys exactly the action of the mind." [14] More than one hundred years ago, William James (1842–1910), the American psychologist, wrote that eye movements might be related to people's thought processes.[15] Almost one hundred years later, in the early 1970s, psychologists discovered that the eyes are not simply receiving visual information. Eye movements help people think and access memorized information. In fact, eye movements appear to be part of the process of accessing information. Consequently, paying attention to people's eye movements will help you understand how they are working with their minds, even though they are totally unaware that they're revealing this information.

Salespeople frequently watch people's eye movements to know whether they are accessing visual, auditory, or kinesthetic information. This allows them to adjust their sales pitch to appeal to their clients' needs, interests, and ways of thinking. These involuntary eye movements are called Universal Eye Patterns.

Universal Eye Patterns are closely related to what we discussed in the last chapter about visual, auditory, and kinesthetic people. However, although a visual person, for example, will talk mainly in visual terms, he or she will also access his or her thoughts with the help of eye movements. The same thing applies with auditory and kinesthetic people. This means his or her eye movements will still reveal the type of memory or thought he or she is accessing.

Right-Handed, Left-Handed, or Ambidextrous

In the next section, we'll be discussing eye movements. I've written the directions for each eye movement for a right-handed person. Most left-handed people will move their eyes in the opposite direction to a

---

14. Ralph Waldo Emerson, *The Conduct of Life* (Boston: Ticknor & Fields, 1860), Chapter V: *Behavior*, http://www.emersoncentral.com/behavior.htm.
15. William James, *Principles of Psychology* (New York: H. Holt and Company, 1890), 193–195.

right-handed person. If, for instance, I say the eyes will move upward and to the left, the eyes of a left-handed person are likely to move upward and to the right. However, there are exceptions. Some left-handed people will move their eyes in the same way as a right-handed person. A few right-handed people will move their eyes in the directions a left-handed person would use. A few ambidextrous people may make some movements in a right-handed person's direction, but make others in a left-handed direction.

This is not a problem once you become used to observing the cues made by people's eyes. If necessary, you can ask a few test questions, and pay attention to where the person's eyes move. With just a little bit of practice, you'll do this automatically.

Visual Eye Patterns (Thinking in Pictures)

Most people visualize something in their minds by looking upward to their left or right. If something is remembered, the eyes will go upward and to the left. If the person is visualizing something he or she hasn't seen before, the eyes will go upward and to the right.

If you visualize the house you lived in as a young child, your eyes will probably look upward and to the left. If I asked you to visualize a lime-green elephant, your eyes are likely to go upward and to the right.

Someone who uses phrases such as "That looks good to me," "I take a dim view of that," or "I see what you mean" is thinking in pictures.

Auditory Eye Patterns (Thinking in Words or Sounds)

People who look horizontally to their left or right side are processing information in the auditory mode. If they look to their left, they are remembering words or sounds they've heard before. My father collected clocks. When I think of them, my eyes go to the left as I recall the sounds they made in the middle of the night when they chimed. If people's eyes move horizontally to the right, they are hearing words or sounds that they haven't heard in that particular way before.

People enter the auditory mode when thinking about answering a question or deciding what to say. Someone who uses phrases such as: "That sounds like a good idea," "That resonates with me," or "That's music to my ears," is thinking in sounds.

Your eyes will move horizontally to the left if you're humming or singing a song to yourself. This is because you're remembering sounds.

Auditory Dialogue

People who look downward and to the left are evaluating something internally. This is self-talk or an internal conversation.

Kinesthetic Eye Patterns (Thinking in Feelings)

People who look downward and to their right are experiencing a feeling or an emotion. They could also be sensing a taste, touch, or smell.

Someone who uses phrases such as: "That feels right," "It's a bit of a stretch, but I grasp the situation," or "I have a sense of what you mean," is thinking in a feeling mode. Naturally intuitive people use this mode regularly.

How to Test Eye Accessing Cues

Ask a friend to help you perform a simple experiment. You will sit opposite him or her and read a series of statements and questions. Your friend should not answer any of them out loud but should merely think about them. You will write down which way his or her eyes move with each of these statements and questions:

1. **Visual Remembered:** Think of the color of your front door. Think of the first person you saw when you left home this morning. Think of the first car you ever owned.

2. **Visual Constructed:** Imagine yourself flying to work. Imagine the head and neck of a giraffe on the body of a hippopotamus. Imagine what your house would look like if it was painted in brightly colored stripes and polka dots.

3. **Auditory Remembered:** Think of your favorite song. Think of the theme of your favorite TV show. Think of the sound of your mother's voice.

4. **Auditory Constructed:** Can you hear the sound of a violin changing into the sound of a pot of boiling water? Imagine a boy soprano suddenly change pitch and sing in a bass voice. Imagine a jet plane sounding like a purring kitten.

5. **Auditory Digital:** Listen to the sound of your own inner voice. What does your inner voice normally say to you? Do you sometimes argue with your inner voice?

6. **Kinesthetic Remembered:** Recall the last time someone congratulated you on something you'd accomplished. Remember the last time someone stroked your face.

Your friend's eyes should have moved in the correct directions for most, if not all, of these questions. It's possible that on one or two of the statements your friend's eyes moved quickly in a variety of directions, rather than just one. This is a sign that what you said overwhelmed the volunteer, and he or she was unable to process it.

Some people use one mode much more than the others. If someone is highly visual, he or she may look upward to the left or right, no matter what question or statement you said. If this occurs, ask the person to tell you what was going on in his or her mind as he or she responded inwardly to the statement.

Once you've finished asking the questions, discuss with your friend how he or she felt during the experiment. If you haven't explained what it was all about beforehand, it's possible that your friend may not have been aware that his or her eyes were telling you what areas of his or her brain were being accessed at any time.

Once you've completed the discussion, swap places, and allow your friend to try the same test on you.

How to Use This Information

Until now, you may have thought that saying, "Your idea *looks* good," is synonymous with saying, "Your idea *sounds* good," and "Your idea *feels* good." In actuality, they are completely different from a psychological point of view.

Watching people's eye movements will help you become a better, more effective conversationalist. Knowing how people are thinking enables you to speak to them in the same mode. If the eyes of the person you are talking with look downward and to the right, you can ask how they feel about whatever it is you're discussing. If the person looks to one side, you might ask, "How does that sound to you?" If the person is looking upward, you might say, "Can I show you something that will make it clearer?"

You need to pay careful attention when asking important questions, as people's eye movements can be rapid. If you're not looking at the other person's eyes while asking the question, the movement may have come and gone before you look.

Talking in the same mode as the other person increases rapport, and it makes him or her subliminally feel that you're both on the same wavelength. Speaking in a different mode is likely to distract and confuse the person you're chatting with.

You need to be aware that observing people's eye movements may not always be 100 percent correct. Someone may look upward (visual), yet say, "It doesn't feel right to me." This happens when the person is visualizing something but is also extremely aware of his or her feelings about whatever it happens to be. When this occurs, you have a choice of using the mode the eyes indicate or the mode the person's words say. It's usually better to go with the mode indicated by the eyes, as the feelings came as a result of whatever it was the person visualized.

Sometimes people's eyes won't move at all. If you ask someone if they've had a good day, they're likely to reply, "Yes, thanks. How was yours?" There's nothing in the question that encourages the eyes to move in a particular direction. In fact, the question and reply are so bland, they're likely to be asked and answered with almost no thought at all.

People's eye movements can also provide clues as to how honest they are. If someone is describing an incident he or she was involved in, his or her eyes should move upward and to the left, showing that this person's memory is being accessed. However, if the person's eyes go upward and to the right, this could be a sign that he or she is inventing or altering some aspects of the story. This may indicate that he or she is lying.

I'm sometimes asked what a blank or unfocused stare indicates. This is a sign that the person is daydreaming or visualizing something. When bringing someone out of that state use visual words.

Facial Expressions

Our facial expressions are extremely revealing. There are seven universal facial expressions that can be found all around the world: happiness, anger, disgust, fear, contempt, sadness, and surprise. (I use a mnemonic to remember these: Here's A Dinner Full of Cold SausageS.) Because these expressions are so readily apparent to others, people often try to conceal them when they don't want others to know what they're really feeling.

Happiness

Happiness is revealed by the eyes, mouth, and cheeks. The lower eyelids rise slightly, and wrinkles appear beneath them. The eyes sparkle, and crow's feet appear at the outside corner of the eyes. The mouth stretches outward and upward. This forces the lines that run from the side of the nose to the corners of the mouth to rise, forcing the cheeks to rise and well outward. Usually, the lips will part to reveal the upper teeth. All of these movements create a warm, genuine smile.

Happiness

Anger

Anger

Anger is revealed by the eyebrows, eyes, and mouth. The eyebrows are drawn down and inward to emphasize the frown lines. The upper and lower eyelids close slightly to narrow the eyes, which stare coldly at the source of the anger. The lips are also compressed and turned down slightly at the corners of the mouth. The nose can be involved, too, as some people flare their nostrils as another sign of their anger.

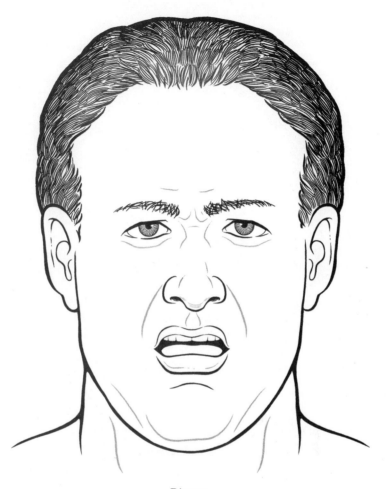

Disgust

Disgust

The eyes, nose, mouth, and cheeks are used to reveal disgust. The lower eyelids rise to create fine horizontal lines immediately below the eyes. The nose wrinkles, causing the cheeks to rise. The upper lip curls and rises in the center.

Fear

Fear

The eyebrows, forehead, eyes, and mouth are used to express fear. The eyebrows rise and pull toward each other. The lines in the forehead become more visible, and they become partly creased in the center. The eyelids rise, revealing the whites of the eyes. The lips are pulled sideways in a straight line. Sometimes the lips part a little.

Contempt

Contempt

Contempt is revealed by the chin and lips. The chin is raised, and the upper lip rises on one side of the face.

Posture

The way people hold themselves provides an immediate clue as to how they are feeling. Someone who is standing tall and straight with head up, feet apart, and arms by the side is feeling confident and in control. Conversely, someone who has his or her arms and legs crossed is probably feeling uncomfortable. Most people know that crossed arms is a sign that the person is closing him- or herself off from whatever is going on. However, like everything else in body language, it can be misinterpreted. The person might be cold, tired, or even using one arm to support the other arm which happens to be sore; I did this when I had tennis elbow. It could even be a habit that the person has unconsciously adopted. Consequently, it pays to observe someone for a while before interpreting their body language. This enables you to see what their body language is like when they are relaxed and free of stress. This is called the person's baseline behavior. Once you've observed this, you're in a good position to notice any changes in body language that he or she makes. If the person you're observing starts making unnecessary body movements, for instance, you'll know that he or she is nervous about something.

In the next chapter, everything that we've already covered will be put into play as we start experimenting with mind-to-mind communication.

*The intuitive mind is a sacred gift and the rational mind
is a faithful servant. We have created a society that honors
the servant and has forgotten the gift.*

—ALBERT EINSTEIN

chapter 5

MIND-TO-MIND COMMUNICATION

Mind-to-mind communication is something people have dreamed about for thousands of years. I hope that by the time you've finished reading and practicing the exercises in this book, you'll be able to send and receive thoughts whenever you wish. Harold Sherman (1898–1987), the American author and psychical researcher, is a good example of someone who was able to do this. One example of his ability was well publicized and documented at the time.

In 1937, a Soviet plane went missing. It had been flying over the North Pole, and it was thought that it had crash landed in a desolate part of Alaska. The Russians asked Sir Hubert Wilkins (1888–1958), a well-known Australian polar explorer, to organize an air search for it. He discussed the proposed expedition with Harold Sherman, a fellow member of the City Club in New York, and they decided to see if they could telepathically communicate with each other on a regular basis.

Harold Sherman agreed to spend thirty minutes, three times a week, at eleven thirty p.m. Eastern Standard Time trying to communicate with the explorer. After each session, Sherman would write down exactly what occurred. These notes were then given to a colleague who could verify, if necessary, that they were written at the time Sherman said they were. Over a period of five months, Sherman made sixty-eight entries that included more than three hundred precise, detailed statements.

Some of these were surprising, considering Sir Hubert was somewhere in the middle of Alaska. On one occasion, Sherman wrote that he sensed Sir Hubert was wearing evening dress and was surrounded by men and women also wearing their best clothes. This was an amazing hit, as at the time Sir Hubert was wearing a borrowed suit and attending an Armistice Ball in Regina. He had been invited to attend this at the last minute. This is just one of the hundreds of telepathic experiences they shared during the search for the Soviet aircraft. Sir Hubert and Harold Sherman later wrote a book about their exploits called *Thoughts Through Space* that is well worth reading.[16]

Both you and your partner in the experiments in this book need to have a genuine interest in mind-to-mind communication. You don't need to be total believers at the outset, as this will come as you start experiencing the reality of it for yourself. However, it's important that neither of you are totally skeptical, as this has been shown to inhibit psychic potential.

An article in *Nature* pointed out that: "If any of those who participate in a physical experiment are tense and hostile, and do not really want the experiment to work, the chances of success are greatly diminished."[17] The best approach is to be open-minded to the possibil-

---

16. H. Wilkins and H. Sherman, *Thoughts Through Space* (London: Frederick Muller Limited, 1971).
17. J. B. Hasted, D. J. Bohm, E. W. Bastin, and B. O'Regan, "Scientists Confronting the Paranormal," *Nature* 254 (April 10, 1975): 470–472.

ity of mind-to-mind communication, but remain cautious and alert to any other possible explanations for your success.

Here are two examples of the need for this. Two people I know were excited, as they seemed to have the ability to send reasonably complicated drawings to each other. I found they could do this only while they were in the same room. Even though they were seated back-to-back, and the receiver was unable to see the movements of the transmitter's pen, she could subconsciously hear the pen's movements as the sender drew her picture. This was enough for her to subliminally receive the drawing. Interestingly, she wasn't aware that this was what she was doing.

An acquaintance of mine was able to name all the cards in a shuffled deck of cards as he dealt them facedown onto a table. When I asked him to use a different deck of cards, he wasn't able to do it. The deck of cards he used was well worn, and he subliminally picked up the minute markings that age and use had created on the back of each card. I must admit that I fooled myself in the exact same way when I was a teenager and first began experimenting in mind-to-mind communication.

These people were not trying to fool anyone. They genuinely believed that what they were doing was psychic, and they were devastated to learn that they had been fooling themselves. Consequently, it's important to check every possibility before telling everyone about your psychic abilities.

Many people become interested in psychic matters after a personal experience of some sort. Hans Berger (1873–1941), the German neurologist and inventor of electroencephalography, is a good example. While undergoing military service, his horse reared, and he ended up in the path of a horse-drawn cannon. The driver managed to halt the horses in time, but Berger was badly shaken by his near brush with death. His sister, many miles away, suddenly felt he was in danger and insisted their father telegram him. It arrived just a few hours after the mishap. This was the only time that Berger ever received a telegram from his father. As a result of this experience, Berger returned to his studies, determined to discover the physiological basis of psychic energy. Between World Wars I and II, he conducted a series of experiments that he believed clearly demonstrated that people could transmit thoughts to each other over long distances.[18]

Choosing the Right Partner

It's important to select the right person, or people, to work with you on your experiments in telepathy. You may be fortunate and already know someone with similar interests to you. I had a school friend named Stuart who was just as fascinated with the psychic world as I was, and we began experimenting together at high school.

Unfortunately, even today, many people keep quiet about their interest in psychic matters. In fact, you may know a number of people with similar interests to you, but as you've never talked about it, neither of you are aware of this. The remedy is to casually mention your interest in mind-to-mind communication and see what response you get. If it's positive, you can discuss the matter further. If the person is dismissive or doesn't want to talk about it, you can simply change the subject.

For many years, I conducted psychic development classes, and many of my students made friends with other people in the different courses I held. At the end of every course, I encouraged my students to continue practicing the various things they'd learned. Some of the friendships made at these classes lasted for years, and I still occasionally meet people who are continuing to develop their skills with the help of friends they met at my courses.

If you don't know anyone you can work with, you might do some research and find out what classes and courses are available in your area. You'll enjoy the classes, and you will meet people with similar

---

18. Brian Inglis, *The Unknown Guest: The Mystery of Intuition* (London: Chatto & Windus, 1987), 94.

interests to you. You may also meet someone who'd make a good partner in these experiments.

You might meet someone in a bookstore or a library. I almost always talk to people I encounter while looking at books in the mind, body, spirit section of libraries and bookstores. Because of your mutual interest, you'll have something to talk about immediately, and if the other person appears to be someone you could work with, you could suggest he or she has a cup of coffee with you to discuss your shared interests further.

New Age bookstores are good places to meet like-minded people. You could mention to the owner of the store that you'd like to meet someone to practice mind-to-mind communication with. He or she would probably be happy to introduce you to other customers with similar interests.

Many New Age stores put on events, such as talks, book signings, and classes. If you attend some of these and make an effort to meet other people there, you may well meet someone you can experiment with. Many of these stores have a notice board to promote New Age events. You might be allowed to place a small advertisement on one of these, asking for someone to work with you on developing mind-to-mind communication skills.

In time, you'll probably meet a number of people you can work with. This is good, as the more people you experiment with, the better. Initially, focus on finding one person you like and whom you feel you can work with. Once both of you start talking about your experiences to others, you'll find you'll quickly start attracting other people. Sometimes, these will be people you would never have considered when you first started.

When I left school, I worked for a large publishing company. They published a wide range of titles, and were, at the time, the world's largest privately owned publisher of religious books. Because of this, I don't think I ever mentioned my interests in psychic matters in the seven years I worked there. One of the other people working there at the same time as me was also keenly interested in the psychic world, but we had no idea we shared this mutual interest until we met up again more than twenty years later. If I'd been looking for someone to experiment with at that time, I would never have considered him.

People who have had a personal experience of some sort make good partners, as they already know that mind-to-mind communication is possible. However, this isn't necessary. Anyone who is willing to suspend disbelief and act on his or her intuition will make a good partner in these experiments.

It's important that you and your partner enjoy the experiments. Consequently, although you must approach the experiments seriously, you should also have fun at the same time. Laugh often and be playful. You should also aim to make your practice sessions reasonably brief, as boredom can set in if the experiments go on for too long. It's better to finish with a desire to do one or two more tests, rather than be thankful that the session is finally over.

Preparation

Initially, you'll find it easier to experiment in familiar surroundings. You need to find somewhere that's warm, comfortable, and safe. This might be a room in your home or the home of the person you'll be experimenting with. Sit down in this room and look around. You don't want to see anything that could be distracting in any way. Clutter is a common cause of this. The room should be vacuumed and dusted also.

You can display anything that you feel might help the experiment. Some people like to hold a crystal or a lucky charm, for instance.

You're likely to feel excited and nervous. This is good, as it's helpful to maintain a sense of anticipation about the experiments you're about to perform.

You might like to have a bath or shower beforehand to symbolically separate the experiments from your normal daily routine.

Wear comfortable, loose-fitting clothes, and have something to eat and drink beforehand.

Temporarily disconnect your phone, and turn any cell phones to silent.

Relaxation

You need to feel relaxed. If you're worrying about something that's going on in your work or home life, you might need to do a relaxation exercise first. There are many ways to do this. Here is a simple relaxation exercise that I enjoy doing.

Lie flat on your back on the floor. Use a pillow under your head, if necessary. Close your eyes and breathe deeply using your abdomen. If necessary, place a hand below your navel to check if your abdomen is rising and falling. Once you've confirmed that you're breathing from your abdomen, take three slow, deep breaths. On each exhalation, say to yourself "relax."

After three exhalations, forget about your breathing and focus your attention on your left foot. Allow it to relax as much as you possibly can. When you feel it is fully relaxed, do the same thing with your right foot. Once your right foot feels relaxed, allow the relaxation to drift over your ankle and up to your knee. Repeat this with your left leg. Continue relaxing your whole body in this way until you feel completely relaxed from head to toe.

After this, focus on your eyes and allow them to relax as much as possible, too. Mentally scan your body to make sure that every part of it is totally relaxed. If you find any areas of tension, focus on them until they let go and relax. Mentally scan your body again to make sure that you are now completely relaxed.

In this state of total relaxation, picture or imagine yourself standing on a bluff overlooking a beach and the ocean. Immediately in front of you is a staircase with ten steps leading down to the beach. Take hold of the handrail and silently count from ten down to one with each exhalation. Imagine yourself doubling your relaxation as you move down one step with each exhalation. When you get down to the beach, lie down on the warm sand and enjoy the feeling of being totally relaxed.

Enjoy the pleasant relaxation for as long as you wish. When you're ready to get up again, slowly and silently count from one to five. Open your eyes, stretch, and after a few seconds, stand up.

Not everyone likes the beach. If you prefer, you could imagine yourself at the top of a staircase that leads down to the most beautiful bedroom you could possibly imagine. Count from ten down to one as you walk down the magnificent staircase. When you reach the bottom, walk over to the comfortable bed and lie down on it. Instead of a bedroom, you might visualize a beautiful, secret room that is furnished exactly the way you want it to be. It contains an incredibly comfortable chair that you can relax in. Whenever you go down the stairs leading to this room, you'll feel totally relaxed and content. If you prefer an outdoor scene away from the sand and the ocean, you might visualize yourself in a beautiful park with the steps leading down to a small hidden grove where you'll feel completely relaxed as you lie down on the beautiful, fresh grass.

Positive Expectations

You should start every experiment with a sense of positive expectancy. You're much more likely to be successful if you expect to be successful. If you feel skeptical or doubt that the experiments will work, you're likely to fail.

The positive expectations should start when you wake up in the morning, even if you're planning to do the experiments in the evening. Feel enthusiastic about what you're going to do. In spare moments, visualize yourself immediately after you've successfully picked up someone's thoughts. Feel the excitement and exhilaration you'll experience.

You can also prepare yourself for the experiments by going through the relaxation exercise. Once you've reached the bottom of the staircase and you're lying down feeling totally relaxed, you can visualize yourself successfully sending and receiving thoughts.

Confidence

You need to have complete confidence in your ability to send and receive thoughts. When you're sending a thought to someone, you must have no doubt in your mind that he or she will receive your thought. Any anxiety or doubt makes success that much harder to achieve.

I find it helpful to imagine the thought leaving my head and flying directly to the mind of the desired recipient. This visualization helps me to focus on the message and the recipient. It also gives me complete confidence in what I'm doing, as I can "see" the thought traveling to the correct person.

Tips for the Sender

Don't try too hard. Focus on the thought you're going to transmit. Visualize yourself putting strength and energy into it and then let it go. In your mind visualize it traveling across the ether to the recipient, wherever he or she may be.

Tips for the Receiver

The best results will come if you remain calm, still, and grounded. If you've ever done meditation, you'll know it's not easy to quiet the mind. Even when you're vitally interested in a conversation, your mind can easily drift off on a tangent, and you fail to hear what's being said. I can remember a number of occasions when I've gone to hear a well-known speaker give a talk on a subject I've been vitally interested in, and I've drifted into a daydream that ended only when the speaker said, "And that was my final point."

Here are some suggestions to help you still your mind while waiting for the sender to send a thought:

- You might visualize yourself quietly relaxing in the place you go to after walking down the stairs in the relaxation exercise.

- You might listen to your breathing. There's no need to alter or control your breath. There's no need to count your breaths, either. Simply be aware of your breathing.

- If you become aware of any extraneous thoughts, gently discard them. I like to mentally push them behind me while thinking, *Out of sight, out of mind.*

Warm-up Exercise

This is an enjoyable exercise that you'll probably continue doing even after you've achieved success with some of the more advanced experiments. Before starting, you and your partner will need to decide who will be the transmitter and who will be the receiver in this experiment. It makes no difference who plays which role first, as you'll take turns at transmitting and receiving.

You and your partner need to sit in two upright chairs facing each other. You need to be close, but make sure that your knees and feet are not touching. Lean slightly forward, if necessary, and clasp your partner's hands. Close your eyes, take a few slow, deep breaths, and then imagine a current of energy flowing down your right arm and into your partner's hand. Visualize this energy continuing up his or her arm, carrying on up through the top of his or her head, and then curving back down his or her right arm and re-entering your body through your left hand. It then flows up your left arm to the top of your head before heading down your right arm again. Visualize this energy circling around and around. As you're imagining this, your partner will be doing exactly the same, creating another, opposite flow of energy. After about sixty seconds you'll experience a powerful connection between you and your partner.

Once you've become aware of this connection, you can take it a step further. The transmitter needs to think of a color and mentally send it down his or her arms on the wave of energy into the hands and arms of the partner. As soon as the receiver gains an impression of a color, he or she should say what it is out loud. The receiver needs to remain alert and say the first thought that comes into his or her mind. Thoughts received telepathically are delicate and ephemeral. Any attempts to analyze or think about what has been received are likely to produce the wrong answer.

If the receiver names the correct color, the roles change, and the original receiver becomes the transmitter. He or she should then send a color to the original transmitter, who is now the receiver. If this thought is picked up successfully, the roles change yet again.

If the receiver fails to pick up the thought of color, the transmitter sends another color, and the receiver tries again. This continues until the receiver successfully picks up the thought, then the roles change.

The experiment continues until each person has succeeded three times.

You should use basic colors until you've gained confidence and proficiency. As your skills develop, you can try unusual colors, such as vermilion, verdigris, and jasper. In the early stages, though, stick to simple colors, such as red, green, blue, and yellow.

Once you've completed the experiment with colors, separate your hands, stand up, and move around for a minute or two. If you feel thirsty, drink some water. You'll have better results if you avoid stimulating drinks, such as coffee or alcohol, until after you've finished.

When you sit down again, visualize the energy surging through your arms and hands into your partner, circling around and around. Once you've reached this state, the transmitter thinks of a number and mentally sends it down his or her arms to the receiver. Initially, this should be a number from one to ten. Later, you can send any number you wish, but you'll progress more quickly if you limit the range in the early stages.

As with the color exercise, the transmitter names the first number that comes into his or her mind. If the answer is correct, the roles change in the same way as before. The numbers are transmitted and received until each person has been correct three times. Once you've both achieved this, get up and walk around again for a few minutes before trying the next stage.

You can carry on with this experiment indefinitely. You might send and receive the names of different fast food establishments, the planets in the solar system, signs of the zodiac, the names of European countries, presidents of the United States, favorite sports, breeds of dogs, and so on.

You'll find, with practice, that you can complete each section of this test in a matter of minutes. The purpose of standing up between each stage is to break the concentration and allow you both to relax. When you start again, you'll feel revitalized and full of energy. You'll also find that you'll be able to visualize the circles of energy more quickly each time you do it.

Although this is an enjoyable experiment, stop when you feel you've had enough. I find about twenty minutes is enough for me. Boredom can be a problem in many telepathy experiments, and this affects the results. It's better to stop while you're still fresh, and then you'll look forward to experimenting with it again.

Energy Transfer Exercise

This is an enjoyable exercise that you can do either on its own or before or after the previous warm-up exercise. In this exercise you and your partner will send bursts of energy to each other.

Start by standing about ten feet apart. For the purposes of explanation, I'll assume that you'll start by sending energy to your partner.

Once you've done that, you can swap places, and your partner will send energy to you.

Both you and your partner should face in the same direction. Close your eyes and visualize as much energy as you can from your body collecting in your heart. When you feel your heart is full to overflowing with energy, open your eyes and raise your right hand over your head with your fingers extended. Take a deep breath, and, as you exhale, lower your arm so your fingers are pointing directly to the center of your partner's back. At the same time, visualize all the energy gathered in your heart shooting down your arm and into your partner's back. You might like to imagine that you're firing energy at your partner with the force of a gunshot. The entire process from lowering your arm and firing the energy should take only a second or two to do.

Your partner is waiting to receive this energy. As soon as your partner feels it, he or she must respond in some way to let you know that he or she received the energy at the moment you sent it. Your partner might say something, turn around, raise both arms in the air, or do anything else to let you know that the experiment was a success.

It might take a few attempts for your partner to feel the energy transfer initially. However, once he or she has become familiar with the exercise, he or she will sense it immediately every time, as the energy is so powerful.

Swap roles once your partner has successfully received the energy to allow you to experience it as well.

In this experiment, you've both been sending energy from your hearts. Once you've both gained experience with this, you can experiment with sending energy from different parts of your body. Try gathering energy in your head or solar plexus, and send that to your partner. Ask him or her if this energy feels different to heart energy. In time, you'll be able to do this without telling your partner what part of your body the energy is coming from, and he or she will be able to feel where it came from.

In time, you'll probably conduct experiments with groups of people. When this happens, you can use this as a group warm-up. Instead of facing away from each other, you should all stand in a circle. One person is chosen to begin. He or she looks across the circle and chooses someone to send the energy to. After gathering as much energy as possible, he or she looks the chosen person in the eye, raises his or her right hand in the air for a moment, and then lowers it and shoots the energy at the selected person's heart.

As soon as this person receives the energy, he or she immediately fires the energy to someone else in the same way. This continues until every person in the circle has received energy at least three times.

This exercise builds up energy and rapport in everyone involved. It's supposed to be enjoyable, so you can laugh out loud while doing it. An acquaintance of mine always clasps his heart and pretends to stagger as soon as he receives energy in this exercise. This adds to the fun and encourages the other participants to improvise and add their personal touches to the warm-up. After a few minutes of this, everyone is fired up and ready to start on the more serious experiments.

Initial Telepathy Exercise

For this exercise, you will need five simple images or designs. Animals or other simple pictures from children's card games are ideal for this. If necessary, you can draw the images on five pieces of paper. If you create your own set of cards, you could draw each one in a different color.

As with all of these experiments, one person will be the sender and the other person the receiver.

When you first try this experiment, you might like to have both people in the same room facing in opposite directions. Sitting back to back is a good way to do this. Alternatively, the receiver could sit in a comfortable chair facing a wall, and the sender could sit several feet away facing the receiver's back. Make sure there are no mirrors or reflective surfaces that might give away clues about the image being transmitted.

The sender mixes the cards and chooses one at random. He or she stares at it for ten seconds and then says that he or she is transmitting it. The sender continues looking at the image and imagines himself or herself transmitting it to the receiver.

The receiver needs to sit quietly and wait until he or she feels or senses an image in his or her mind. When this happens, he or she should tell the sender, who then tells the receiver if he or she is correct.

The sender mixes the cards again, chooses another card at random, and again transmits it telepathically to the receiver. This is repeated three or four times and then the roles reverse, with the sender becoming the receiver.

The best results come if you treat this test as a light-hearted game rather than a serious experiment. Laughter produces much better results than grim determination. Consequently, you should stop doing this test while it is still fun. As soon as it starts feeling like work, your success rate is likely to drop.

You should keep a record of your successes and failures. Repeat the exercise every now and again over a period of months.

You're quite likely to find that one person is better at, say, sending than receiving, while the other person might be equally as good (or as bad) at both. There's no need to worry about this, as your results at both sending and receiving will improve with practice.

You should also try this experiment with as many different people as possible. There is one proviso. The people you experiment with must, at the very least, be open-minded about the possibility of mind-to-mind communication. If someone doesn't believe it's possible, his or her negative beliefs will adversely affect the outcome. Initially, you'll probably find that the best results come when you do these experiments with open-minded family members.

Daily Routine Exercise

This is an interesting exercise to do with a friend or a family member who is open to the possibility of mind-to-mind communication. Tell this person that at some time on the following day you'll send him or her a thought. If this person picks it up, ask him or her to call, text, or e-mail you.

At some time during the next day, ideally at a time when you would not normally be thinking of this person, you need to stop doing whatever it is you're doing and focus on him or her. Think about how much you care for this person and send thoughts of love. You might find it helpful to look at a photograph of the person as you transmit your thought.

Hopefully, this person will contact you to confirm that he or she received your thought. However, as you're sending the thought during the day, you might have sent it at a time when the person was too busy or focused on a task to receive the message. It's possible that he or she received your thought but was unable to contact you right away. You'll be able to find out if your thought was received when you speak to your friend later on in the day.

Once you've succeeded with this, ask the other person to send a thought in the same way to you.

You can take this exercise a step further by not telling the other person what day of the week you'll be making contact telepathically.

Drawing Experiment

For this exercise, the sender and receiver should each gather a pad of paper and a pen or marker. Then, both should sit down and relax. At a pre-determined time, the sender draws a simple design on his or her pad. A star, flower, boat, or house are examples of suitable pictures to start with. He or she focuses on the drawing and mentally transmits it to the receiver. He or she must feel totally convinced that the receiver will pick up the thought. When the receiver picks up an impression, he or she also draws it on a pad. The whole experiment can be completed in two to five minutes.

The two people should then change roles to give both participants the opportunity to be both sender and receiver.

It takes practice to become good at this. However, rather than repeating it dozens of times in a single evening, it's better to stop after, say, twenty minutes, and perform the experiment again at another time. Once both of you have gained proficiency with this, the drawings can become more elaborate.

Family Telepathy

This experiment is something you can try anytime you're sitting at home with other family members or good friends in the room. Choose the person you're going to send the thought to. Do not look at him or her, but silently send that person a thought. You might telepathically ask him or her to get you a glass of water, for instance. You might simply let the person know how much you love him or her.

Keep thinking along these lines for three or four minutes, or until the person responds in some way. If you requested a glass of water, for instance, the person might get up and get it for you. However, it's more likely that he or she will ask you if you want something or say something along the lines of "I'm getting a glass of water. Would you like one, too?" If you're sending thoughts of love, the person might turn to look at you and smile.

Turn Around

In the introduction, I mentioned how I used to focus on the person sitting in front of me at school and will him to turn around. Once I'd succeeded with him, I'd focus on someone else, and I'd gradually work my way around the class. A few months ago, my wife and I were attending a show at a comedy festival. I happened to notice someone whom I hadn't seen since my school days sitting several rows in front of us. I focused on the back of his head and willed him to turn around. About a minute later, he turned around and we waved to each other. During the intermission we had a chat, and he told me that he knew it was me, as he'd experienced the same sort of sensation he'd felt when I sent him the same thoughts in class more than fifty years earlier. It's interesting that he remembered the feeling after such a long time.

You can do this experiment anytime you're with a group of people. Start experimenting with friends and acquaintances who are facing away from you. Look at the back of their heads and send them thoughts along the line of "Turn around, Bill (or whatever the person's name is). I'm looking at you. I'm focusing on you right now. Please turn around and acknowledge me." Keep on sending thoughts in this vein until the person looks around, usually with a slightly confused look on his or her face.

After you've had several successes with friends and acquaintances, try doing this with strangers. It might take a little longer to get them to turn around, but if you persist, you'll find they will.

Hand on Head Test

This is a simple experiment that can be done anywhere. Ask your partner to look around the room you're in and mentally choose an object he or she can see. Place your hand on your partner's head and ask him or her to concentrate on the object. It's important that he or she doesn't give the game away by staring at, or even glancing at, the selected object. There's no need to try to think of the object he or she chose. Simply remain relaxed and passive, and see what comes into your mind. When you feel you know what the item is, let go of your partner and walk around the room. Pick up the object that you were drawn to and ask your partner if you were correct. If you were, change roles and do it again. If you failed to pick up the right object, try it again and again until you select the right item.

Once you've successfully done this experiment a few times, try doing it without making physical contact with your partner.

Instead of choosing an object, your partner could think of an emotion or a simple instruction, such as "Go and stand by the door." I find this considerably harder than thinking of an object, but I have met a number of people who find this variation easier to do. Experiment and see which version is more challenging for you.

Eye Test

This is an interesting test that involves gaining impressions from someone else's mind. You and your partner sit facing each other. Your knees don't need to be touching, but you need to be close enough to gaze into your partner's eyes. This sounds easy, but many people find it hard to gaze into someone else's eyes for any length of time.

Obviously, you shouldn't glare at your partner. Instead, look deeply into his or her eyes with a caring, compassionate gaze. He or she should do exactly the same with you. Neither of you should speak. Simply gaze into the other person's eyes and see what comes into your mind.

You may not receive anything the first few times you do this. If you receive nothing, stop after five minutes, and try again on another day. You'll find, with practice, that you'll start to sense exactly what is going on in the other person's mind as you gaze into his or her eyes.

Once you stop, ask your partner what he or she was thinking to see if it confirms the impressions you received. Naturally, you need to tell your partner what you were thinking as well.

Once you develop your skills at this, you'll find it useful in everyday life. You will, for instance, be able to tell if someone is lying or telling the truth when he or she is talking to you. You'll also be able to pick up the person's feelings about whatever topic he or she is talking about.

With all of these experiments, the person you're working with needs to be present. In the next chapter, this isn't necessarily the case, as we'll be experimenting with sending and receiving thoughts over the phone and by e-mail and text messaging.

The odds against this [telephone telepathy] being
a chance effect are 1,000 billion to one.
—DR. RUPERT SHELDRAKE

chapter 6

EXPERIMENTS OVER THE PHONE

Most people have had the experience of knowing who was on the other end of the phone before answering it. If you ask a group of people if they've ever experienced mind-to-mind communication, the chances are that most of the people who have will say it occurred with a phone call. The phone rang and they instantly knew who it was, or maybe they thought about someone and shortly afterward received a call from him or her. Experiences such as these occur most frequently with family members and close friends.

The earliest experience I can remember of an incident of that sort occurring to me was when I was nineteen and living in a city five hundred miles away from home. It was the first time I'd been away from home for any length of time. Late one Sunday evening the phone rang, and I knew instantly that my younger sister, Meredith, had died. There was no reason for me to suddenly know this. Yet, before getting out of bed to answer the phone, I knew what had happened. I had obviously picked up the thought from one of my parents.

I've also had the more pleasant experience of thinking about some-one and deliberately willing him or her to phone me. Almost always, the person I'd been thinking about would phone in response to this. This is not uncommon, as I've met many people who've also done this successfully. It seems many people deliberately do this to encourage the other person to contact them.

When my mother was alive, she used to phone me at five p.m. every day. Obviously, I didn't have to be psychic to know who was on the other end of the line when my phone rang at that time. However, on one occasion, the phone rang at five p.m., and before answering it I told my wife that I thought it was an old school friend calling me. Much to her—and my—surprise, I was correct. My friend lived several thousand miles away, in a different country, and I had no idea he was back home visiting his family. I wasn't thinking about him, but he must have been thinking about me before picking up the phone. My only regret was that I wasn't brave enough to greet him by name when I answered his call.

Rapid advances in technology mean people are experiencing telepathy in many other ways, too. You might, for instance, know who sent you an unexpected text message or e-mail before checking the device.

Before the invention of the telephone, telepathy was a valuable way to contact people living far away. In the late nineteenth century, when people started seriously researching the psychic world, numerous case studies were recorded of people receiving telepathic messages from relatives and friends who lived in different parts of the country. Many of these were verified by independent witnesses.

There are also many recorded instances of people thinking of some-one and then receiving a letter from that person a day or two later. Mark Twain (1835–1910), the American humorist and author, spoke about this in a letter he wrote in 1884:

> I have reaped an advantage from these years of constant obser-vation. … I have been saved the writing of many and many a let-ter by refusing to obey these strong impulses. I always knew the

other fellow was sitting down to write when I got the impulse—
so what could be the sense of us both writing the same thing?
People are always marvelling that their letters "cross" each other.
If they would but squelch the impulse to write, there would not
be any crossing because only the other fellow would write. I am
politely making an exception in your case. [19]

Examples of this sort are still reported from time to time, but the
telephone and other communication devices mean telepathy is often
the last way people try to contact someone, rather than the first.

The telephone is, oddly enough, a useful device for encouraging
telepathic messages. When someone decides to call someone, he or she
will think about the other person, possibly look up the phone number in
a directory or on the Internet, and then make the call. During this time,
the person is clearly focused on whomever it is he or she wants to speak
to, and this makes it possible for that person to receive thoughts about
the caller before he or she makes the call.

Virtually everyone has had the experience of knowing who was on
the other end before picking up the phone. This may well be because
of the focus and concentration of the person who has made the call.

Many people have the ability to think of someone and have the
person phone them several minutes later. Often they'll say, "I was just
thinking about you" or "I had an urge to phone you," not knowing
that the person they'd phoned had set the wheels into motion by his

---

19. Mark Twain, "Letter to William Barrett," *Journal of the Society for Psychical Research*
    1 (1884), 166–167. Mark Twain was an early member of the American Society for
    Psychical Research and recorded a large number of his own psychic experiences.
    Here's an example of one of them. In 1875, it occurred to Mark Twain that some-
    one should write a book about the Nevada Silver Mines. Although he hadn't seen
    William H. Wright for twelve years, he thought Wright would be the perfect per-
    son to write the book. He immediately wrote an outline that he intended sending
    to Wright. It then occurred to him that he should interest a publisher in the project
    before writing to Wright. Before he could do this, he received a letter from Wright
    saying that he was thinking of writing a book on the silver mines and did Twain
    think it was a good idea.

or her thought. Of course, sometimes this may be simply coincidence, but as this is such a common experience, it's unlikely that every example can be explained as simply chance or coincidence.

Modern technology provides even more ways to test mind-to-mind communication. I regularly e-mail my older son in London, and I often receive an e-mail from him within seconds of sending mine. We were both thinking of each other and writing our e-mails at the exact same time. I don't consider these to be telepathic, as we exchange messages regularly and usually e-mail each other at about the same time of day.

However, I have had experiences that may well be telepathic. A short while ago, I e-mailed an old friend in Scotland. We see each other about once a year, and we usually exchange e-mails only on birthdays and at Christmas. On this occasion, my wife and I talked about him over breakfast. When I went upstairs to check my e-mails, I decided to send him a brief message. I spent about ten minutes writing it, bringing him up-to-date with our news. I sent it, and less than sixty seconds I later received a long, newsy e-mail from him. He wrote that he'd just happened to think of me and decided to send me an e-mail. I can think of no explanation, other than telepathy, to explain that. There was no reason for either of us to e-mail each other, yet we both thought about the other at the same time, and we both decided to write an e-mail.

Dr. Rupert Sheldrake, the remarkable English researcher, author, and parapsychologist, and his co-researcher Leonidas Avraamides conducted a study to see if people can successfully know who sent them an e-mail before they receive it. Interested people provided their e-mail address, along with the e-mail addresses of three friends who had agreed to take part in the experiment. All four people received an e-mail that thanked them for participating in the experiment and explained how it worked. A few minutes later, a computer randomly chose one of the participant's three friends and sent him or her an e-mail, asking the person to send an e-mail reply to the message that would be forwarded on to the participant. The friend was also told not to contact the participant until after the test was over. Once the friend sent back a reply, the computer automatically sent an e-mail to the participant saying that a friend had sent him or her a message, and would he or she please reply with a "guess" as to which friend had sent it. The participant replied to this, and after it had been received, the computer automatically sent the friend's e-mail to him or her. This experiment was repeated either six or nine times, with up to a five-minute delay between trials.

As you can see, the entire process was automated. The computer chose the friend and the length of time between each trial. Because the tests were all done by e-mail, the exact time that each stage took place was clearly documented.

The experiment was a success. Out of 419 trials, 175 correct guesses were made. The success rate was 41 percent, which is significantly more than the chance score of 33 percent (as there were three friends in each test, the odds were one in three). Interestingly, when the time delay was increased from up to five minutes to longer than ten minutes, the success rate increased slightly to 45.6 percent. However, if the delay was between three and ten minutes the results were about the level of chance (32.1 percent).[20]

The One Week Test

All you need for this experiment is an exercise book, a pen, and a phone. Turn off or cover up any form of caller identification you may have. For one week, each time your phone rings, think about who could be on the other end before you answer it. After the phone call is ended, write down your findings. Record any hunches or intuitions you had before answering the phone and any feelings you had about what the call was likely to be about. Do not include expected calls in

---

20. Rupert Sheldrake and L. Avraamides, "An Automated Test for Telepathy in Connection with E-mails," *Journal of Scientific Exploration* 23 (2009): 29–36, http://www.sheldrake.org/files/pdfs/papers/JSE_Vol23.pdf.

this experiment. In my case, I would not have recorded my daily five p.m. conversation with my mother, for instance.

At the end of the week, analyze your results and see how successful you were. I suggest doing this for one week, but in practice I sometimes do it for several weeks at a time. It's a simple and enjoyable exercise that makes you realize how much mind reading occurs over a device that is designed to eliminate the need for it.

Telephone Test

You will need to involve four friends to help you perform this test. At some stage before the time of the phone call, they have to decide which of the four will call you. At the designated time, this person will phone you. Before answering the phone, you need to decide which friend is calling. This means you answer the phone by saying, "Hello, Janet (or whoever you think it will be)." Alternatively, before answering the phone, you can tell someone who is with you the name of the person you think is calling.

The person who phones you should focus on you for a few minutes before making the call. You should prepare for the call by making sure you're comfortable and relaxed at least fifteen minutes before the time of the call. The odds in this test are one in four, or 25 percent.

However, when Dr. Sheldrake experimented with this using 63 subjects at Goldsmith's College in London, the results achieved were 40 percent in 570 trials, showing that something other than pure chance was involved. Similar results were achieved when the same experiment was performed at universities in Holland and Germany. Later, when Dr. Sheldrake repeated this experiment on British television using five sisters who were all members of a band called the Nolan Sisters, the results were 50 percent.[21]

---

21. Rupert Sheldrake, "Telepathy in Connection with Telephone Calls, Text Messages and E-mails," *Journal of International Society of Life Information Science (ISLIS) Vol. 32*, (No. 1, March 2014), http://www.sheldrake.org/files/pdfs/papers/ISLIS _Vol32.pdf. See also: Rupert Sheldrake, *The Sense of Being Stared At and Other Aspects of the Extended Mind* (London: Hutchinson, 2003), 95–121.

Telephone Test Variation

This variation of the previous test is an experiment you can try with a group of friends. One person receives the phone calls and "guesses" who is calling before answering the phone. He or she can remain at home for this experiment. The other people gather together in one of their homes. At a pre-determined time, one of them rolls a die, and the number on top indicates the person who'll make the call. If you have six people in the room, each person is given a number. If you have, say, four people in the room, each is given a number from one to four. If the die rolls a five or a six, it's simply rolled again until a number from one to four appears.

The person the die indicates calls the friend, and he or she has to be brave enough to say, "Hello, Jennifer (or whoever they think the person is)," when answering the phone. The results are recorded.

The test can be repeated every five minutes and stopped after ten phone calls have been made.

You might like to experiment with this by starting with two possible senders, and after achieving success with that, gradually increase the number of possible senders. If you have two senders, the person making the phone call can be chosen by tossing a coin.

E-Mail Test

This test is similar to the Telephone Test. Again you'll need four friends. Ideally, you'll also need a fifth person to direct the test. Let's assume one of your friends will send you an e-mail at three thirty p.m. Fifteen minutes before this time, the person directing the test contacts one of your four friends and asks him or her to send you an e-mail at three thirty p.m. The other three people do not hear from the person directing the test, and this tells them they have not been chosen on this occasion. The person who is chosen thinks of you for a few minutes before three thirty p.m. and then sends you an e-mail. One minute before then, at three twenty-nine, you need to send the director an e-mail telling him or her which person you think will be sending you an e-mail.

The purpose of all this is to provide clear evidence of what has happened, as each e-mail will have the time and date recorded on it. As with the earlier experiment, the chances of success are one in four, or 25 percent.

Please Call Me

You've probably thought about someone and then received a phone call from him or her shortly afterward. Sometimes these people will say they had a sudden urge to call you or that you'd been on their mind and they thought they'd give you a call. In this experiment, you'll send a telepathic message to a friend or family member asking them to call you.

You can try this mind-reading exercise with anyone you know. The good thing is that they don't necessarily have to know you're doing it. In this exercise, you sit down in a comfortable chair, relax, and mentally ask a specific person to phone you. Initially, you should try this with the person who has been your partner in the previous experiments. Once you've had some success, and gained confidence, you can mentally ask other people to contact you.

The best time to do this is in the evening, or at any other time when you think the person you're contacting will be relaxing. Start by thinking about the person you've selected for this experiment. Sit down comfortably, close your eyes, take several slow, deep breaths, and then visualize the person as clearly as you can. If possible, see in your mind's eye what he or she is doing at that moment. Picture the person stopping what he or she is doing and walking to a telephone. Visualize him or her phoning you. See how happy he or she is when the call goes through and he or she can talk to you. Take three deep breaths, and each time, as you exhale, silently say, "Phone me. Phone me now." Think about your friend for a few minutes, and then say to yourself something along the lines of: "I need you to contact me. Please phone me now. I'm at home, waiting for your call. Please phone. I must talk to you now. Please (whatever the person's first name is), phone me. It's important that you call me now." Continue talking to yourself in this vein for about five minutes.

You may find the person calls you within a few minutes. However, it may not be possible for him or her to call you right away. He or she might be in a meeting, at a movie, or be sound asleep, for instance. Remain alert to the possibility that the person might respond to your thought telepathically and send a thought back to you. He or she might also respond in a different way from the one you expected. Although you asked him or her to call you, the person might respond by sending you a text message or an e-mail.

If you receive no response that day, repeat the exercise for the next three or four days. Hopefully, the person will contact you within that time. If you receive no response at all, phone the person for a chat. Don't mention your experiment until the person has had time to tell you his or her news. You may find that he or she had been thinking about you but hadn't got around to making a call.

Don't give up if the experiment didn't work with the first person you tried it on. Select someone else, and see if you have better luck with him or her.

While you're practicing this with your partner, you might start out by saying you'll contact him or her on, say, Wednesday afternoon. This gives you both a time frame for you to send your thought. When your partner hears it, he or she needs to contact you as quickly as possible. Once you've both done this successfully, you can expand the time to include an entire day. Once you can do this, you can then do the exercise whenever you wish, with no prior arrangement.

The final step is to telepathically contact friends and family and see if you can cause them to phone you using nothing but the power of your thoughts.

In the next chapter, we'll replicate some of the experiments performed by Dr. J. B. Rhine at Duke University using playing cards and ESP cards.

In a word, then, we have to face not only the fact
of the actual existence of extra-sensory perception:
we have to accept it as another normal process along with the rest—
simply less understood than some.
—DR. J. B. RHINE

chapter 7

EXPERIMENTS
WITH CARDS

When I was about sixteen years old, a friend and I started using play-ing cards to try to demonstrate telepathy, clairvoyance, and precog-nition (predicting the future). I'd found a copy of Dr. J. B. Rhine's monumental *New Frontiers of the Mind: The Story of the Duke Experi-ments* in the school library, and Stuart and I decided to test each other to see how psychic we were. My parents played bridge, and we used their discarded old and worn decks. This wasn't ideal, as sometimes certain cards were easy to identify from the backs. This didn't worry us initially. It was only when we started keeping records that we used pocket money to buy new decks of cards. I also made my own deck of ESP cards, which I drew on the back of my father's business cards.

Before discovering Dr. Rhine's book, we'd been using the cards for card games and gambling. Stuart and I became so fascinated with our experiments in ESP that we forgot all about card games and poker.

From time to time, we'd allow other friends to participate in the experiments, but none of them lasted long. Some of them thought we were decidedly weird, and they couldn't understand our fascination with the subject. Others enjoyed the initial experiments, but they became bored, as we were inclined to go on for too long.

We continued the experiments, off and on, for about three years, until Stuart left home to go to college. Unfortunately, I lost the records we kept many years ago. I've no idea how it happened, but I've managed to keep one of the decks of cards we used, and it brings back many happy memories whenever I see it.

The first scientific tests that used playing cards to test for psychic ability took place at Stanford University, Palo Alto, California, between 1913 and 1917. John E. Coover (1872–1938), an assistant professor of psychology at the university, used 97 senders and 105 receivers, most of whom were students, in more than one thousand experiments. The card-testing experiments involved the color, suit, and number of the cards. The court cards (jack, queen, and king) were not used.[22]

Dr. J. B. Rhine, generally considered the "Father of Modern Parapsychology," was appointed instructor of psychology at Duke University, North Carolina, in 1928. Professor William McDougall, his chair, encouraged him to explore the field of parapsychology. Dr. Rhine's subjects spent countless hours transmitting the images of ESP, or Zener, cards to someone on the other side of a screen.[23] There are twenty-five cards in a deck of ESP cards: five each of a cross, square, circle, star, and wavy lines. Dr. Rhine had some significant early successes, but gradually the volunteers' results dropped as they lost interest in the experiments.

---

22. John Edgar Coover, *Experiments in Psychical Research* (Stanford, CA: Stanford University, 1917).

23. ESP cards are sometimes called Zener cards. This is because they were created in the early 1930s by Karl Zener (1903–1964), a perceptual psychologist, to test extrasensory perception. Karl Zener spent most of his career working with Dr. J. B. Rhine at Duke University in Durham, North Carolina.

Dr. Rhine's major problem was that his volunteers started with a great deal of enthusiasm, but they soon became bored with the guessing procedure. Basil Shackleton was a volunteer in a similar series of experiments conducted in the United Kingdom. When he gave a lecture to the Society for Psychical Research sometime later, he pounded the table and screamed: "I was bored, bored, BORED!"

Another person who had the same problem was Eileen Garrett (1893–1970), sometimes referred to as the "greatest" psychic of the twentieth century. When Dr. Rhine conducted a series of card-reading tests with her in 1934, her results were no better than chance. She was puzzled by this, and she decided that her poor results were the result of boredom. She had no sense of personal involvement, and, as she wrote: without "the emotional keys which I felt were necessary to unlock the door of my sensitivities" she was unable to produce good results. Eileen Garrett eventually achieved excellent results with Dr. Rhine's card-reading experiments, but these came only after she'd visualized "an active emanation between two people or between an individual and an object." She claimed that the cards "lacked personality," but once she started focusing on the minds of the people transmitting information to her, rather than focusing solely on the cards, her scores increased dramatically.[24]

Because focusing on cards for lengthy periods of time can be tiring as well as boring, it's important to have some sort of reward at the end of the experiment. This doesn't need to be anything major, but it should be something you enjoy doing, such as visiting a café for tea or coffee, going for a walk, or meeting up with friends.

Another problem with scientific experiments is something called the experimenter effect. This demonstrates that the way in which the participants are treated has a significant effect upon the outcome of the experiment. Someone who is considered to be nothing more than

---

24. Eileen Garrett, quoted in Elizabeth Floyd Mayer, *Extraordinary Knowing: Science, Skepticism, and the Inexplicable Powers of the Human Mind* (New York: Bantam Books, 2007), 196 and 267.

a number will not do as well as someone who is considered a partner or colleague in the experiment.

The personal biases of the people conducting the experiments also play a significant role. Someone who has a desire to find out if telepathy is real, but actually doubts that that is the case, will inevitably produce results that confirm his or her beliefs. Another experimenter who knows that telepathy exists because he or she has experienced it, will produce results that confirm the reality of mind-to-mind communication. This is called the "sheep-goat effect." It was discovered in 1942 by Dr. Gertrude Schmeidler, professor of psychology at City University of New York. She designed a questionnaire to determine the views her students had about extrasensory perception. Once they'd completed the questionnaire, she gave them a series of tests using ESP cards. When she compared the results of the test with the questionnaire, she found that the people who believed in ESP (the sheep) achieved results significantly greater than chance. The other students (the goats) did the exact opposite; they produced results significantly below the chance level.[25]

Another problem Dr. Rhine found was that different forms of ESP were closely connected. If someone was capable of naming cards at above the chance level while someone else was looking at them, it would be considered an example of telepathy. A similar experiment would be called clairvoyance if the person being tested could do the same thing while no one was looking at the cards. It would be an example of precognition if someone could name the order of a deck of cards at above chance level before the cards were mixed.

This seems straightforward, but in actuality it wasn't quite that easy. It's possible for someone being tested to pick up the identity of the cards clairvoyantly, rather than receive them telepathically from the person who was transmitting them. A clairvoyance test could be

---

25. Gertrude Schmeidler, "Predicting Good and Bad Scores in a Clairvoyance Experiment: A Preliminary Report," *Journal of the American Society for Psychical Research* 37 (1943): 103–110.

an example of predictive telepathy if the subject managed to read what was going on in the mind of the experimenter as he or she checked the order of the cards afterward.

Because of the potential confusion this could cause, Dr. Rhine devised "pure telepathy" experiments. In these, the sender thought of cards in a random order, rather than looking at actual cards. To ensure the order was completely random, the senders used lists of numbers that they converted into cards using a code that they had remembered, as it wasn't written down. After the receiver wrote down the identity of the card, the sender wrote down what he or she had sent. This method worked extremely well. Dr. Rhine wrote: "The result of all the comparisons was that there was no essential difference in the scoring rate, whether the pure telepathy type of test or the old-style procedure of undifferentiated ESP was used."[26]

Dr. Rhine was unfairly maligned throughout his career by critics saying he hadn't done enough to prevent the possibility of fraud. Every time he was criticized, he used it as an opportunity to see if his controls could be improved. In many cases, they could be. When, for instance, people complained that the person shuffling the cards might be inadvertently cueing the person being tested, Dr. Rhine replaced the human shuffler with a machine. He also took steps to remove all means of contact between the experimenters and the volunteers who were being tested. When his statistical procedures were questioned, Dr. Rhine asked the American Institute of Mathematics to thoroughly investigate the methods he and his colleagues were using. In 1937, the American Institute of Mathematics declared that their uses of statistics were totally valid. No one was ever again able to question his integrity.

Replacing the Cards in the Deck

In the 1980s, Fabrice-Henri Robichon, a French doctor, read about the work conducted by Dr. J. B. Rhine, and he decided to do some

---

26. J. B. Rhine, *New World of the Mind* (London: Faber & Faber, 1954), 24.

experimentation himself. He made a special deck of ESP cards for the experiments. The crosses were red, the squares black, circles yellow, stars green, and the wavy lines blue. This made the cards more interesting than the standard ESP deck in which all the symbols are printed in black.

The other major change he made was with the selection of the cards. In previous tests, the cards were mixed and the sender transmitted all the cards in order from the top to the bottom. In Dr. Robichon's tests, the cards were shuffled and the sender took out any card from the deck. He transmitted this to the receiver. The card was then replaced in the deck, and the cards were mixed again before another card was taken from anywhere in the deck.

The advantage of this is that the person receiving the thoughts had no idea how many cards of each symbol would be transmitted to him or her.[27] This is known as the "replacement" method, and it is the method that is now routinely used in scientific experiments using cards of any sort.

Dr. Robichon experimented mainly with twins. His most remarkable results came with a series of experiments he did with male twins who were twenty years old. In his report, he commented slightly ruefully that their best results (92 percent success) came when they were "semi-drunk."

Probabilities

When parapsychologists started using playing cards and ESP cards in their experiments, they also needed to work out the probabilities for each possible result. For instance, if someone is transmitting the color of a playing card, the odds are fifty-fifty, as the answer has to be either red or black. No matter how many cards have been dealt, the odds for each individual card remain at fifty-fifty. However, it's possible for sev-

---

27. Fabrice-Henri Robichon, "Monozygotic Twins and Telepathic Phenomenon," French Review of *Psychotronic Vol. 02*, No. 1 (1989): 19–35.

eral black cards, for instance, to appear one after the other. This could affect the results temporarily, but after a reasonably long run of "card guessing" experiments the result will always be approximately fifty-fifty, as the law of averages comes into play. If someone manages to get a better result than chance would indicate over a series of experiments, it's a sign that something other than chance is influencing the outcome. This something is likely to be mind reading.

Determining if a card is red or black is an easy test compared to going through an entire deck of fifty-two playing cards and naming each card. If you successfully managed to name the top card, the odds are fifty-one to one that you'll be able to name the second card, fifty to one that you'll successfully name the third card, and so on. If you manage to name all fifty-two cards, you will have beaten odds of "fifty-two factorial," written as "52!", which is a number containing sixty-eight digits. This number is approximately eighty thousand billion, billion, billion, billion, billion, billion, billion, billion, which is considerably more than the number of grains of sand on every beach in the entire world.[28] It's unlikely that you'll ever telepathically receive the names of fifty-two cards in a row, but, in the same way that people win the lottery, it could happen.

However, let's assume you're transmitting the colors of playing cards to a friend, and he gets seven out of ten correct. At first glance, this appears to indicate that your friend is truly psychic. A parapsychologist needs to determine the chances of this result occurring. With the first card there are two possible outcomes: red or black. There are four possible outcomes when the second card is added to the equation: red-red, red-black, black-red, and black-black. In a run of ten cards there are 1,024 possible combinations of outcomes. If your friend was purely guessing at the outcome each time, there are only 210 different ways in which he could have successfully guessed seven out of ten cards.

---

28. Michael Kaplan and Ellen Kaplan, *Chances Are …: Adventures in Probability* (New York: Penguin Books, 2006), 64–65.

The chance of this result occurring is 210 divided by 1,024, which is slightly over 20 percent. This is a good result, but not enough on its own to be considered an example of ESP. The test would need to be repeated a number of times before a parapsychologist would agree that something out of the ordinary was occurring.

Experiments with Playing Cards

Regular decks of playing cards are easy to find, and they are a good choice for a variety of different tests. If you remove the jokers, you'll be left with fifty-two cards, twenty-six of them black and twenty-six red. Start by giving the cards a thorough mix. Unfortunately, the casual shuffles most people use when playing card games are not very effective. A good way to ensure a good mix is to spread the cards facedown on a table, mix them, and then pick them up one at a time in a random order, selecting them from all over the table. If possible, the cards should be mixed out of sight of the receiver. This eliminates the possibility of him or her accidentally seeing one or two cards while they're being mixed.

I have described these experiments using two people: a sender and a receiver. However, if you know a number of people who are interested in mind reading, you can use as many people in these experiments as you wish. You may, for instance, have several people sending the information to one receiver. You might have one person sending information to several receivers. You might have four senders and four receivers. Even if you know several interested people, you might choose to work with each of them on a one-to-one basis. You'll find some people are naturally better at sending thoughts, rather than receiving them, and others will be the opposite. Usually, people who think they'll be better at one half of the experiment than the other will produce results that bear out their assumption. It's fun to try different combinations and to compare the results you receive when working with different people.

Red or Black

You and your partner can sit facing each other when you first experiment with this. Once you've gained experience, you should sit facing away from each other, as you don't want the receiver to pick up any involuntary changes in facial expression the sender may make.

The sender sits with the shuffled, facedown deck in front of him or her. He or she takes the top card and looks at it, making sure the receiver doesn't get a glimpse of it. He or she gazes at the card for a few seconds and then looks at the receiver and imagines sending the color to him or her.

The receiver says what he or she thinks the card is, and is then shown the card. If the color is correct, the card is placed to the transmitter's left. If the color is wrong, the card is placed to the right.

The transmitter then takes the next card and attempts to send its color to the receiver. This card is also placed to the left or right, depending on whether or not the receiver was correct.

This process continues until the color of all fifty-two cards have been transmitted.

It's easy to determine how successful the receiver has been by counting the cards on the left-hand side. The chance score is twenty-six correct, as the odds of a pure guess are one in two. However, if the receiver gets, say, thirty-two or thirty-six correct, the result may be significant, although these results would need to be produced regularly over a series of tests.

After this, the cards are mixed again. The test is repeated with the roles reversed: the sender becomes the receiver, and vice versa.

Unless both participants are feeling fresh and motivated, the test should stop after both people have had an opportunity to be both sender and receiver. It is better to stop before you're ready, rather than continue until you are both exhausted. This eliminates the drop-off in results that boredom creates.

You should repeat the experiment when you both feel ready for it. If you wished, you could do it again after a break of a few hours, but you'd probably get better results if you tried it again on another day.

Once you've performed this experiment a few times, you can make some changes and see if they affect the results. The most important one is to face in opposite directions, so you cannot see each other. This eliminates any inadvertent visual cues that the sender may provide. It also means the receiver can't see the growing pile of successful cards and make guesses, or informed decisions, about the remaining cards based on the number of cards in the pile.

This doesn't eliminate any aural cues. The sender still has to tell the receiver when he or she is transmitting the color of a card. Despite his or her best intentions, the timbre of his or her voice may change slightly when saying a particular color. This isn't likely, of course, but if you want your experiments to be totally legitimate, you need to eliminate any possible cues. Only then can you be assured that the results are obtained by sending and receiving thoughts.

You can eliminate the voice by having the sender ring a bell or make any other mechanical sound to tell the receiver that he or she is sending the thought. I usually use a drinking glass and a spoon. When I gently tap the spoon on the side of the glass, the receiver knows that I'm about to send the thought. Another method is to synchronize the second hands on both participants' watches. The sender can then send a thought at pre-agreed times, such as every fifteen, twenty, or thirty seconds.

Once you've experimented a few times with these increased limitations, you can add a final check. The receiver says out loud what he or she picks up. The sender makes no response to this. Instead, he or she records it on a pad. The cards are all dealt facedown into a single pile. After all fifty-two cards have been transmitted, the receiver can turn around. The results are checked by turning over the pile of cards, which means the first card dealt is now at the top of the pile. If the color of this card matches what is written on the pad, a tick is placed beside it. After all the cards have been checked, the ticks are added up to provide the result.

A more scientific way of checking the results is to use a sheet of paper or an exercise book. I prefer using school exercise books, as this keeps the results in a single place, and it's possible to look back over a period of time to see how the receiver is progressing at developing his or her telepathic abilities. Draw two vertical columns. Label the left-hand one "Sent" and the right-hand column "Received." When the sender sends out a thought, he or she writes down what it is in the "Sent" column. When the receiver calls out what he or she thinks the card is, the sender records this in the "Received" column. When the run of cards is exhausted, the results are checked to see how well the receiver did.

If you're performing these experiments with a specific goal in mind, such as a serious attempt to develop your abilities, you should write down your results. If you're doing a run of cards purely for fun, this isn't necessary, but even then I think it's a good idea to record the results. This is because our memories are fallible, and it can be hard to remember exact results weeks or months later.

Hearts, Clubs, Spades, or Diamonds

The next stage is to double the number of choices. Instead of transmitting red or black, the sender has to transmit one of the four suits in a deck of playing cards. This is done in exactly the same way as the previous experiment. The two people sit facing away from each other and use a bell or some other signal to advise when the suit is about to be transmitted. The results are not checked until all the cards have been sent.

If the bell rings loudly enough, or the two participants have synchronized their watches, the two people can sit in different rooms, as distance makes no difference in telepathy. On one occasion, I participated in this experiment with a friend on the other side of the world.

We used a telephone and calibrated the second hands on our watches. Once the phone call was over, we started at a predetermined time, and I transmitted a card to my friend every fifteen seconds. We then repeated the experiment with him sending thoughts to me. We had performed this experiment a number of times when he was staying with me in New Zealand, and I was keen to find out if our results would be better or worse when we were twelve thousand miles apart. Our results were much the same, showing that the thousands of miles between us made no difference at all.

One to Ten

This is a much more challenging test. The court cards (jack, queen, and king) are removed from the deck, leaving the forty numbered cards (ace to ten). These are thoroughly mixed, and then the transmitter sends the number of the card to the receiver. Obviously, the odds are one in ten each time. If you consistently do better than this, it's a sign that your telepathic skills are developing.

You can expand this test by including the court cards; jacks would be eleven, queens twelve, and kings thirteen.

One Red Card

This is my favorite telepathic test using playing cards, as it's one of the tests Stuart and I used to do when we were teenagers. You need several black cards and one red card. The cards are thoroughly mixed and laid out in a facedown line across a table. The cards should be separated from each other by at least the width of a card. While you are in a separate room, or have turned your head away, your partner looks at each card so that he or she knows the position of the red card.

Once the sender has done that, you hold a hand a few inches over the card at one end of the row and slowly move your hand across the line of cards from one end to the other. While you are doing this, your partner telepathically tells you to stop when your hand is over the red card. Continue moving your hand over the cards from one side to the other until you feel a strong desire to turn over a particular card. You don't need to hurry with this. Take your time. If the urge to turn over a particular card is not particularly strong, continue along the line and see what happens when you return to that card. Sometimes, you may sense the word *stop*, while at other times you'll feel as if a strong magnet is pulling you down to the red card. When you feel confident in your choice, lower your hand and turn over the card.

If you're successful, swap roles and allow your partner to have a turn. If you haven't succeeded, try four more times, and then change places.

This experiment is a wonderful way to introduce people to the concept of mind reading, as you can do it with a large group. Explain the procedure, and then leave the room while everyone sees where the red card is. When you return, run your hand slowly over the line of cards. Ask everyone to think *stop* when you are over the correct card. Once you've successfully demonstrated this, you'll find all of your guests will want a turn too. Not surprisingly, the more people present, the easier this experiment is to do.

Ten Times Five

In this experiment, the receiver tries to pick up the one card that the sender is thinking of in a group of five cards. Start by removing two cards from a shuffled deck of cards. One of these should be the ace of spades. This leaves fifty cards in the deck. The ace of spades is removed as it is a particularly obvious card, and is likely to be chosen for that reason. The other card is removed to create a deck of fifty cards.

The fifty cards are arranged into ten packets, each containing five cards. Any cards that might prove confusing in one pile are placed into another. This occurs if two cards of the same number appear in one pile. The seven of spades and the seven of clubs are an example of this.

All the piles are placed facedown on a table. One pile is selected and the five cards in that packet are placed faceup in a line across the table. The sender looks at the cards and mentally selects one. He or she then stands behind the receiver and projects the name of the card as he or she looks at them. When the receiver decides which one it is, he or she names it and finds out if the "guess" was correct.

This is repeated with the other nine piles. Statistically, the receiver should name the correct card twice in a run of all ten packets, as the odds are 20 percent, or one in five.

The cards can be mixed again, and the test repeated with the sender and receiver changing roles. However, as this experiment is mentally tiring, a reasonable amount of time should elapse before the sender and receiver repeat the experiment without changing roles.

The Lie Detector

This is an enjoyable game that will help you develop your intuitive skills. In everyday life, this game will also help you determine if someone is telling you a lie. All you need is a deck of playing cards, a pen, and paper. It can be played with two or more players.

The first person to get a certain number of points wins the game. Ten is a good number to start with. However, you may want to increase this once everyone is familiar with the game.

Only the dealer can score points. However, as the dealer changes after every round, everyone has the same opportunity of winning the game. The initial dealer can be chosen by any method you wish. A common way of doing this is for the participants to each take a card from the shuffled deck. The person who picks the highest value card becomes the first dealer.

The dealer mixes the cards again and deals a card facedown to every participant. Each player looks at his or her card, but they make sure no one else sees it. Once everyone has looked at their card, the dealer turns to the participant to his or her left. Let's assume this person is Bill. "What is your card, Bill?" the dealer asks. Bill does not need to correctly name the card he was given, as he can either lie or tell the truth.

Let's assume Bill has been dealt the queen of clubs. However, as he does not need to name this card, Bill might, for instance, say, "seven of diamonds." The dealer has to decide if Bill is lying or telling the truth.

Let's assume the dealer felt that Bill was lying. "You're lying," he says. Bill then shows his card, which confirms that he was lying. Because he "guessed" correctly, the dealer gets a point.

The dealer then repeats this with the other participants. We'll assume the second person is Julia, and she was given the two of hearts. When the dealer asks her to name her card, she says, "two of hearts." If the dealer decides she was lying, he would not get a point. This is continued until the dealer has asked each person the name of his or her card. His total of correct "guesses" is written down, and the deck is passed to the person on the dealer's left. This person becomes the new dealer, and he or she starts the new round. The new dealer shuffles the cards, deals a card to each player, and starts asking questions.

Process of Elimination

This is a fascinating test, as it involves the receiver avoiding the mentally selected card. While the receiver is out of the room, the sender deals six cards faceup in a row on a table. He or she chooses one of these to be the target and then turns all the cards facedown.

The receiver comes into the room, and the sender tells him or her the name of the target card. The sender stands behind the receiver and thinks of the target card and its position in the row. He or she also wills the receiver to avoid that particular card.

The receiver turns over cards one by one, trying to avoid the target card. Obviously, the best result occurs when the receiver manages to turn over all five indifferent cards. However, it's also a sign of success if he or she manages to turn over four cards before turning over the target card, especially if this can be repeated a number of times.

Extrasensory Perception Cards

In the early 1930s, Dr. J. B. Rhine asked Karl Zener, a perceptual psychologist and a long-time colleague, to design a deck of symbol cards that could be used for testing psychic abilities. They were originally called Zener cards, but nowadays most people call them ESP cards. A deck of ESP cards contains twenty-five cards, five each of five symbols: a circle, wavy lines, a plus, a square, and a star. They are available at most New Age stores. As magicians sometimes use ESP cards in their magic shows, they are also available at magic stores. They can also be bought online.

In his book *Extra-Sensory Perception*, Dr. Rhine describes experiments he made with ESP cards using an undergraduate student named Adam Linzmayer. On May 21, 1931, Linzmayer correctly named the first nine cards in a deck of ESP cards. The odds against this occurring are approximately two million to one. On a later occasion, Dr. Rhine took Linzmayer for a drive in his car to help him relax. They stopped the car and conducted an informal test. Linzmayer succeeded in getting fifteen cards correct in a row. The odds against this are more than thirty billion to one.[29]

Amazingly, Linzmayer was not Dr. Rhine's most outstanding subject. That honor goes to Hubert Pearce, a divinity student, who managed to average ten out of twenty-five correct cards on his first five thousand attempts. On one occasion, Pearce succeeded in naming twenty-five cards in a row correctly. The odds against this occurring are 298,023,223,876,953,125 to one! Interestingly, Pearce did not usually succeed with long runs of hits. However, on this occasion, Dr. Rhine offered him one hundred dollars for each card he named cor-

29. J. B. Rhine, *Extra-Sensory Perception* (Boston: Boston Society for Psychic Research, 1934), 59–64, http://www.sacred-texts.com/psi/esp/esp12.htm.

rectly. This obviously motivated Pearce, who made $2,500 from the experiment.[30]

ESP cards were devised to create a set of symbols that had no symbolic meanings. For instance, many people consider the queen of hearts to be the card of love and the ace of spades the card of death. ESP cards have no emotional connotations.

If you have already experimented with the tests using playing cards, ESP cards add an additional symbol you can send and receive.

There are two ways to do this. The deck is thoroughly mixed. In Dr. Rhine's first experiments with ESP cards, the cards were mixed by hand. Later, he switched to card-shuffling machines to make sure the cards were genuinely mixed. Once the cards have been thoroughly mixed, the sender transmits the symbols in the usual way. The receiver calls out what he or she has received, and the results are checked once all twenty-five cards have been transmitted.

The problem with this is that there are five cards of each symbol in the deck. Consequently, the receiver might realize he or she has called out, for instance, the circle five times already. If he or she senses another circle, should he or she say "circle" or choose another card?

The remedy for this is to have each card replaced in the deck, which is then reshuffled before the next card is transmitted. The procedure takes considerably longer, but the sender always has a choice of five different symbols to transmit each time. This means the sender has to record the card transmitted, as well as the card the receiver names. After doing this twenty-five times, the experiment is over, and the roles of the two people reverse.

Again, these experiments should be performed in a cheerful, positive manner, concluded before either participant becomes bored.

---

30. J. B. Rhine, *New Frontiers of the Mind: The Story of the Duke Experiments* (New York: Farrar & Rinehart, 1937), 94, http://archive.org/stream/ newfrointersofth028563mbp/newfrointersofth028563mbp_djvu.txt.

Other Types of Cards

Varying the types of cards you use is an excellent way to eliminate the boredom factor. Many years ago, I made my own set of color cards by attaching squares of different colors to blank cards. You can buy decks of blank playing cards from magic dealers. However, nowadays, it's also possible to create your own decks of cards online.[31] This means you might, for instance, create a deck of thirty-five cards, five each of the seven colors of the rainbow. You could create a deck of animal cards, photos of friends and family, places in the world you'd like to visit, and so on. Now that you can produce one-off decks at reasonable prices, there's no limit to the number of different decks you can have.

You might find it interesting to create a deck containing strong emotional associations. In the 1950s, two psychic researchers found a subject who was extremely good at receiving crosses and circles when being tested with ESP cards. He was not nearly as good at receiving the other three symbols. When he was questioned about this, the man said he associated the cross and the circle with male and female sexual organs. The researchers created a special deck of cards that replaced the cross and the circle with male and female symbols. In 240 trials, the man was highly successful at receiving these, but achieved only chance levels with the other symbols. The difference between the erotic and nonerotic symbols was pronounced.[32] This shows that cards containing emotional associations can, in certain circumstances, be easier to transmit and receive.

One man I knew many years ago related the ESP symbols to food. He visualized the circle as a pizza, the plus sign as an Easter hot cross bun, the wavy lines as streaky bacon, the square as a cake, and the star as a platter containing candy. His mother had a star-shaped plate that

---

31. If you do an Internet search for "self publish playing cards," you'll find a wide selection of companies who'll be happy to make a single set of cards for you. One possibility is www.thegamecrafter.com.

32. G. W. Fisk and D. J. West, "ESP Tests with Erotic Symbols," *Journal of the Society for Psychical Research* 38 (1955–56): 1–7.

was used to hold candy at Christmastime. He found his results improved enormously when he starting sending and receiving thoughts of food, rather than unemotional symbols. This is similar to the need Eileen Garrett had to create some sort of emotional connection between her and the ESP cards to achieve good results.

Controls

If you're practicing these tests with a number of people, you need to have controls in place to eliminate the possibility of cheating. Most people are honest and wouldn't deliberately cheat. However, every now and again, someone does. This is probably because they want to feel the admiration of others who are not doing as well as they apparently are. No matter what excuse they provide, you should refuse to include these people in future tests. This is because having done it once, there's always the possibility that they'll do it again.

Any reflective surfaces, such as mirrors and even cups of coffee, should be removed or placed out of sight of the receiver.

It's advisable to use new, or nearly new, decks of cards. This is because all cards, through use, get slightly marked. Someone who wants to cheat could use these almost invisible marks to gain a better result. However, more often, these slight marks are picked up subliminally, and the person isn't aware that he or she is using them. Either way, the results are affected. This is yet another reason why the cards should be kept out of view of the receiver.

Experiments with cards are fascinating. However, they have a major drawback in that the personal element has been removed. One person in one room telepathically transmits the design of an ESP card to someone in another room. Even if he or she can consistently do this at well above the chance level, it's not mind reading as most people view it.

"Real" mind reading, as most people see it, occurs between people in a personally significant way. For most people, real telepathy occurs when someone who is in danger telepathically contacts her father half a world away, and he is able to help. This creates an experience that neither person could ever forget. Unfortunately, despite the many thousands of experiences of this sort that have been recorded, scientists can't accept them because they cannot be replicated.

In the next chapter, we'll move on to some more advanced experiments that involve "real" mind reading.

The average number of correct guesses is five out of twenty-five. As the number of correct guesses grows, so do the odds against chance playing a part in it grow also. The element of clairvoyance or extra-sensory perception comes into play.

—DR. J. B. RHINE

chapter 8

MORE ADVANCED EXPERIMENTS

If you've had some success with the previous experiments, you're ready to move on to some more advanced tests. I think you'll find them both interesting and challenging.

You can expand the playing card experiments in chapter 7 indefinitely. Instead of sending the color or suit of a card, for instance, you might transmit the whole card. There are two ways in which the sender can transmit this information. If the card is, for instance, the three of hearts, the sender could focus on this and try to send the name of the card to the receiver. Alternatively, he or she could do it in stages, starting with the color, followed by the suit, the number, and finally the entire card. The second method is usually more successful, as the receiver can pick up the information one step at a time, and each new piece of information helps him or her build up a picture of the complete card.

You can also expand the distance between the sender and the receiver. If you and your mind-reading partner live in different homes, you can experiment by sending a thought at a predetermined time. Once you've had some success with this, you can try sending your partner thoughts at different times of the day. You need to keep a record of when you send a message, and the receiver also has to note the time he or she received it. With this particular test, it's common for the receiver to suddenly become aware of the sender, but receive nothing more than that. This is not a failure, if the sender was transmitting a thought to the receiver at that particular time.

Photographs

I used to use postcards in my mind-reading experiments, and I bought them every time I traveled anywhere. Nowadays, that isn't necessary, as it's possible to download interesting photos from the Internet that are perfect for mind-reading experiments. You can also find interesting photographs and illustrations in books and magazines. You can use any pictures you wish, but I've found the best ones to start with are:

- Photos of objects or scenes that are easily recognizable, such as the Taj Mahal, the Eiffel Tower, or the Grand Canyon

- Photos from nature, such as a spider's web, a seagull in flight, an elephant, or a snake

- Photos of interesting shapes, such as the pyramid entrance to the Louvre, an orange, or the Petronas Towers in Kuala Lumpur

- Photos that capture happy or emotional moments, such as an elderly person in a rocking chair, a small child walking and holding hands with a grandparent, a small boy with his dog, or a soldier meeting a loved one after a long absence

- Photos of people and/or animals that both the sender and the receiver know

All of these are relatively easy to send and receive. Here are some experiments using photographs.

One in Five

You will need five photographs or drawings for this experiment. Ideally, all of the photographs should be as different as possible from each other. You might, for instance, choose one photograph each from the five groups listed above.

Both the receiver and the sender know what photographs will be used in the experiment. The photographs are placed into opaque envelopes, which are then mixed. One envelope is selected, and the photograph inside it is then transmitted to the receiver. This process ensures that the sender transmits a genuinely random photograph, rather than selecting a personal favorite. If the sender decides on a particular photograph beforehand, he or she could inadvertently send it to the receiver before the experiment started. If possible, ask a third person to place the photographs into the envelopes, mix them, and select the one that will be used.

If the receiver stays in the same room as the transmitter, he or she must face away to avoid the possibility of accidentally seeing the photograph. By this stage, you've learned that distance makes no difference to telepathy, and there's no need for both sender and receiver to be in the same room, or for that matter, city or country.

The sender concentrates on the photograph and sends it telepathically to the receiver. The odds are one in five for this test, the same as the experiment in the previous chapter using ESP cards.

Once the receiver has experienced some success with this test, it can be made more interesting. The sender mixes up the envelopes containing the photographs and places them in a stack in front of him or her. He or she then looks at the photograph in the first envelope, and transmits it to the receiver. The receiver records what he or she picks up. Once this has been done, the sender looks at the photograph in the next envelope and transmits that. This continues until all five photographs have been sent. Only then are the results compared.

This experiment can be made even more difficult by replacing the photograph into its envelope after it has been transmitted to the receiver. All five envelopes are mixed again, and an envelope is chosen. This is done five or ten times in a row. By doing it this way, the same photograph may be transmitted two, three, or even more times in the one test.

One in Fifty

You'll need a large number of photographs for this test. I use fifty, which is why I call this test *One in Fifty*. The photographs are thoroughly mixed, and one is chosen. This might be the top photograph in a facedown stack or a photograph pulled from the middle of the stack at random. The sender concentrates on it, and he or she sends it to the receiver. This is repeated until the transmitter has sent the number of photographs that was decided on before the test began.

This test is considerably harder than the One in Five experiment, as the larger number of photographs that can be chosen mean the receiver can't "guess" the result.

If desired, the stack of photographs can be mixed between each transmission.

Pure Telepathy

I've called this experiment Pure Telepathy as neither the sender nor the receiver see the photographs ahead of time. A third person is asked to bring ten interesting illustrations or photographs to the session, and these are what the transmitter sends to the receiver.

On one occasion when I was experimenting with this test, a friend brought a large book of photographs by a well-known photographer. Another person present was asked to name ten numbers, and the photographs on those pages were transmitted to the receiver.

This experiment might not sound any more difficult than One in Fifty, but in actuality it is. Even when fifty photographs are used, the receiver and sender gradually become familiar with them. This means the receiver knows that the only photographs being transmitted are in the group of fifty, and automatically discards any impressions that don't relate to them. If he or she receives an impression of a barn owl, for instance, but knows there is nothing like that amongst the fifty photographs, he or she will discard the thought and wait for something else to appear in his or her mind.

Dice

Dice have been used for gaming and gambling purposes for thousands of years. The oldest known dice are between four and five thousand years old.[33] Gamblers regularly try to perform psychokinesis with them by willing a die to roll to a particular number. This has been tested scientifically with mixed results.[34]

A typical die has six different faces, providing six possible outcomes. You should roll a die from a dice cup or other small container rather than from your hands. In scientific tests involving dice, a barrier of some sort is used. The die is rolled from the cup to the table, where it bounces against the barrier before coming to rest on the table.

Fifty-Fifty

This test is similar to guessing the color of a playing card, as the odds are one in two. The sender rolls a die, looks at the number on top of it, and transmits this to the receiver. There are two possibilities: an odd or even number, or a low (1, 2, 3) or a high (4, 5, 6) number. This test is repeated ten times, and then the roles change.

---

33. *Burnt City, Key to Lost Civilization*. Press TV, April 11, 2007, http://edition.presstv .ir/detail/5668.html.

34. Leonid L. Vasiliev, *Mysterious Phenomena of the Human Psyche* (New Hyde Park, NY: University Books, 1965), 174.

One in Six

Again a die is rolled, but this time the sender transmits the number on top of the die. Again, ten trials are conducted before the two people change roles.

You can make these dice experiments more challenging by increasing the number of dice that are used. With two dice, the sender could transmit the total of the two numbers appearing on top of the rolled dice, or he or she could send each number separately.

Drawings

It's a simple matter to evaluate the results of telepathy tests using playing cards, ESP cards, and dice. However, it's much harder to do this with drawings and photographs. In fact, it can usually only be done when the range of drawings and photographs is severely restricted. Not surprisingly, the name for tests of this sort is "restricted-response tests." The experiments become much more interesting in free-response tests, as there is no limit to what the item being transmitted may be.

In his book *Mental Radio*, Upton Sinclair (1878–1968), the American novelist, described a series of free-response experiments he and his wife, Mary Craig Sinclair, performed. Upton Sinclair drew pictures of objects that were randomly selected and attempted to transmit them telepathically to his wife. Over a period of time, he transmitted 290 drawings. She successfully picked up 65, and she achieved partial success with another 155. The remaining 70 were failures. This is a remarkable achievement. There is no way to evaluate their results statistically, but the remarkable successes the couple achieved provided convincing evidence of their abilities.

Whately Carington (1892–1947) was a British parapsychologist who became interested in psychic subjects after World War I. He was interested in the ESP card experiments conducted by Dr. J. B. Rhine. He felt that quantitative experiments of that sort demonstrated that ESP exists but failed to provide information on the nature of it. "The use of drawings as test material offers … an enormously greater chance than does the use of cards, etc., of finding out something about the kind of thing that is going on," he wrote.[35] He devised a number of experiments using drawings and tried to evaluate these statistically.

Carington's most famous experiment with drawings lasted ten days. Each day he selected a random page number in *Webster's Dictionary*, and the first object on that page that could be drawn became the target. His wife made a sketch of whatever it was, and at seven p.m. he hung it up in his study. It remained there until nine thirty the following morning. The people he was testing drew what they thought he was transmitting in a ten-page sketch pad. Each ten-day test was considered one experiment. After a group of experiments, Carington shuffled all of the drawings and sent them to an outside judge to evaluate. Carington conducted eleven of these experiments, and in the process he collected 20,000 drawings.

Carington was unusual in that he refused to accept any drawing as a hit if it was interpreted differently, even if it matched the drawing being sent. If, for instance, a drawing of an orange was transmitted, an identical picture labeled "peach" by the receiver would be considered incorrect.

Carington's results were significantly higher than chance. He found that his receivers did not necessarily need drawn pictures, as they were also able to pick up images in his mind that he transmitted to them. He also discovered a precognitive effect. Most of his receivers gained their impression on the night he was focusing on them, but a significant number received the image a day earlier or a day later.[36]

---

35. Whately Carington, "Some Observations on the Experiments with Drawings," *Journal of Parapsychology* 4 (1940): 131.

36. Whately Carington, "Experiments on the Paranormal Cognition of Drawings," *Journal of Psychical Research* 4 (1940): 1–129.

Other Items

Anything at all can be transmitted telepathically from one person to another. If the success rate of an experiment declines, it can be a good idea to use something else for a while. You might experiment with smaller or larger objects to see if variations in size affect the results. Changes in color and texture could also be considered.

Dr. K. Ramakrishna Rao, the Indian philosopher and parapsychologist, found some subjects scored better when coins, rather than marbles, were transmitted. This could be because coins are considered more valuable than marbles. He also found that children do better when transmitting and receiving simple objects they are familiar with, rather than more complicated or unfamiliar items. This is because they're interested in things that are familiar, but they become frustrated with more complicated items.[37]

The Drink Test

This is an interesting experiment in which the person being tested attempts to telepathically identify the drink that someone else is drinking. The drinks should vary, and ideally should be nonalcoholic. Possible drinks include tea, coffee, milk, tomato juice, cordials, and a selection of sodas.

The person being tested takes a glass of water into another room. Once he or she has left the room, the person doing the tasting pours a drink and slowly drinks it. At the same time, the receiver slowly sips the glass of water and attempts to pick up the name of the liquid the sender is drinking. The drinking action of the receiver helps him or her gain an impression of the particular drink that is being consumed. Frequently, rather than gaining a mental image, the receiver will identify the correct drink from the water, as it will seem to "taste" of the drink the sender is consuming.

---

37. K. Ramakrishna Rao, *Experimental Parapsychology: A Review and Interpretation* (Springfield, IL: Charles C. Thomas, 1966), 79.

This experiment can also be done with different types of food and confectionery.

Multi-Aspect Targets

Multi-aspect targets are items in which two or more characteristics need to be identified to determine the entire picture. A red rose is an example. In the previous chapter, one of the tests with playing cards involved identifying the color, the suit, and the number.

It can be difficult to evaluate the success of tests of this sort. Obviously, the ideal result occurs when the receiver picks up all the details, and says, "it's a red rose" or "it's the seven of diamonds." However, you'll find some people will be good at picking up, say, the colors of objects, while others might sense the object, but not "see" any colors.

G. L. Mangan, a parapsychologist, recorded an experiment utilizing color and form. His subject scored extremely well for both in the first half of the experiment but achieved significant results for the color only in the second half.[38] Some people are naturally good at seeing the color and form together, as they are intrinsically connected to each other. Other people have to determine first one aspect, and then the others, one at a time.

Multi-aspect experiments can be extremely difficult. Two researchers conducted an experiment with fifty-five volunteers who were sent one- to five-digit numbers. The subjects successfully picked up the first and last digits, but missed on the inner digits.[39]

---

38. G. L. Mangan, "An ESP Experiment with Dual-Aspect Targets Involving One Trial a Day," *Journal of Parapsychology* 19 (1955): 35–44. See also: J. E. Kennedy, "Information Processing in ESP: A Survey of Forced-Choice Experiments Using Multiple-Aspect Targets," *Journal of Parapsychology* 44 (1980): 9–34, http://jeksite.org/psi/jp80.pdf.

39. C. B. Nash and M. G. Durkin, "Terminal Salience with Multiple Digit Targets," *Journal of Parapsychology* 23 (1959): 49–53.

Another interesting multiple-aspect experiment using numbers is to transmit two numbers to the receiver. He or she then has to add these numbers and record the answer.

Quotes and Jokes

This is an interesting experiment that can be done whenever you wish. My partner and I used to do this whenever either of us thought that our interest levels were declining.

The first step is to gather a collection of famous quotations and sayings that you both like. You can include proverbs, one-liner jokes, and even full-length jokes. Copy these onto individual file cards. To perform the experiment, the sender thoroughly mixes the facedown file cards and places them on the table. He or she takes a card randomly from the middle of the stack. The sender then focuses on the saying and transmits it to the receiver.

My partner and I both enjoy risqué jokes, and we found they were easy to transmit and receive. I think this is because the humor inherent in the jokes appealed to both of us, and this must have helped the transmission and receiving process. Funnily enough, we both gained an additional benefit from this exercise, as it helped us memorize our favorite jokes.

Sometimes we sent and received nothing but jokes. This proved to be an excellent way to recapture interest after a lengthy session. Usually we used a mixture of sayings, proverbs, quotes, one-liners, and jokes to ensure there was plenty of variety in the experiment.

Four Boxes

This experiment requires four large identical cartons, and at least twenty objects, such as toys, household items, food, stationery—anything that can easily fit inside one of the boxes.

In this experiment, the receiver leaves the room. The sender chooses four items from the collection of objects and places one in each of the four boxes. All the other items are put out of sight. The four boxes are placed in a straight line on a table. Ideally, each box should be at least a foot away from the others. The sender selects one of the four items in the boxes as the target. If you have a third person to help, he or she can mix up the four boxes, so even the sender doesn't know which box the target item is in.

The receiver is invited into the room. The sender concentrates on the item, trying to send a mental picture of it to the receiver. The receiver is able to walk around the table and hold his or her hands over the different boxes to see if any impressions can be gained from them. It's possible that the receiver will sense the identity of the object, but it's more likely that he or she will pick up that it's an item of fruit or a child's toy. Any impressions of this sort are good, as the aim of the experiment is not to identify the object, but to determine which box the target item is in. Once he or she has decided which box the item is in, the receiver touches it. The box is then opened to see if he or she is correct.

The roles are then reversed, to give each person a turn as both sender and receiver.

After you and your partner have been practicing this experiment for a while, you can make it considerably more difficult by having a third person gather the required items. As well as determining what box the item is in, you also have to pick up the identity of the selected object. In this test, neither the transmitter nor receiver know what any of the items are until afterward.

Invisible Picture

This experiment involves the sender creating a picture or an image in his or her mind and transmitting it to the receiver. The receiver can either draw whatever it is he or she receives, or alternatively, describe what he or she picks up.

The receiver sits quietly in a room with a pad and a pen nearby. He or she closes their eyes and waits until an image or a picture comes to mind.

At the same time, the sender also sits quietly in another room with eyes closed. After taking several slow, deep breaths, he or she starts to think of an image, a word, or a shape. The sender focuses on it until it is clear in his or her mind. When he or she reaches this state, he or she thinks of the receiver and transmits the thought. There is no need for the sender to strain or force the sending in any way. It's much better to send the thought slowly and gently. I like to send the thought on each gentle exhalation to enable the receiver to pick up the thought as a series of impressions in his or her mind. I also visualize the thought traveling to the mind of the receiver.

When the receiver gains an impression of what is being sent, he or she picks up the pad and pen and writes or draws what was received. It's important that he or she write down what was received, no matter how strange or ridiculous it may seem. Many receivers doubt what they're receiving, and they try to analyze the thought. This effectively kills all chance of success, as the process is based on feelings and sensations, rather than logic.

This is a more difficult experiment than the other exercises in this chapter. This is because the receiver can choose literally anything to transmit. Because most people tend to think of simple objects to transmit, it can be helpful to browse through a number of books and magazines containing interesting and colorful photographs to gain ideas.

The sender should transmit two or three thoughts to the receiver before they are checked for accuracy. Both sender and receiver should pause for something to eat or drink before changing places and repeating the experiment.

Despite the difficulty of this exercise, some people find it easy to do, and they can't understand why others have to practice it over and over again to gain the expertise they naturally possess. There's no need to be concerned if your partner is naturally better than you are at picking up thoughts with this, or any other, experiment. With practice and regular experimentation, you'll develop the same skills.

Painful Experiment

Despite its name, this experiment is neither dangerous nor particularly painful. In this test, the transmitter lightly pricks him- or herself with a pin or a needle. If you don't have access to either of these, a sharp pinch will work just as well. The receiver should telepathically feel a sensation in the same part of his or her body. Usually, this is a sense that this is the place where the transmitter pricked himself or herself. However, some people who are particularly sensitive can experience mild pain, as if they also had been pricked in that particular spot.

There have been many reported instances of twins doing this involuntarily. If one twin hurts their right leg, for instance, the other twin, who could be many miles away, may feel a sensation, or even pain, in the same place at the same time.

The Community of Sensation Test

In the late nineteenth century, Alfred Russel Wallace (1823–1913), the British naturalist who is best known for his work on the theory of evolution, and William Barrett (1844–1925), the physicist and a pioneer in psychical research, found that people who were hypnotized reacted to the actions of the hypnotist. If the hypnotist pricked himself with a pin, for instance, the hypnotized person would rub the same area on his or her body. Likewise, if the hypnotist tasted something bitter, the hypnotized subject would react with an expression of distaste. These tests became known as "community of sensation." These experiments can also be done without hypnosis.

For this experiment, you'll need to obtain a variety of substances, such as salt, sugar, pepper, nutmeg, and cloves, that you can taste or smell. Make sure the receiver is far enough away to prevent him or her from smelling whatever it is you are experimenting with. Place a small amount of one of the substances in your mouth. The receiver should be able to detect what it is almost simultaneously. Place the other substances in your mouth, one at a time, to see if the receiver can detect all of them.

Ganzfeld Experiment

Ganzfeld is a German word that means "whole field." It's a technique that was developed in the 1930s by Wolfgang Metzger (1899–1979), a German psychologist, but it wasn't until the early 1970s that three investigators, all working independently, started conducting serious experiments into telepathy with it. These investigators were Charles Honorton (1946–1992), from the Maimonides Medical Center's dream laboratory; William Braud (1942–2012), associate professor of psychology at the University of Houston, Texas; and Adrian Parker, associate professor of psychology at the University of Gothenburg, Sweden.

Wolfgang Metzger found that when volunteers gazed into a featureless field of vision, they usually hallucinated. People who are trapped underground for periods of time usually experience hallucinations, too, as they're deprived of the sense of sight and the brain tries to regain it without success. Ganzfeld experiments use sensory deprivation to enable the nervous system to become aware of faint telepathic messages that might otherwise be overlooked. It's a fascinating experience.

In a ganzfeld experiment, the receiver is placed in a state of information deprivation for thirty minutes. During this time, the sender sends thoughts to him or her. The receiver says out loud what he or she is receiving, and these comments are recorded. At the end of the process, the receiver is shown four possible targets, one of which is the one the sender tried to transmit. Consequently, the chance rate is one in four.

In the early 1970s, Honorton, who had been working on dreams and ESP at the dream lab at Maimonides Medical Center, started experimenting with the ganzfeld. He felt that minor sensory deprivation would increase the possibility of psychic contact between two people. He published the results of his first experiment into this in 1974. The ganzfeld process has been developed considerably since then, and it is still one of the main methods being used by scientists to study mind-to-mind communication.

From 1974 to 1981, forty-two experiments were conducted using the ganzfeld method. Of these, 55 percent produced positive results, with a success rate of 38 percent, which is considerably more than the expected chance rate of 25 percent. By 2004, eighty-eight ganzfeld experiments had been conducted with a success rate of 32 percent. The odds of this result occurring by chance are twenty-nine million trillion to one.[40]

Most people enjoy experimenting with the ganzfeld. Although scientific experiments using this are computerized nowadays, it's a simple matter to replicate the original experiments.

You'll need a Ping-Pong ball that is cut in half, a comfortable recliner-type chair, a source of red light, a set of headphones, and a recording of white or pink noise. I prefer pink noise, as it sounds like a waterfall.[41] If you can't obtain these, a recording of static will work just as well. You'll also need a selection of ten or more photographs to act as the targets. If the receiver feels nervous and needs to relax before the procedure, you'll also need a pleasant relaxation tape for him or her to listen to before the experiment begins.

---

40. Dean Radin, *Supernormal: Science, Yoga, and the Evidence for Extraordinary Psychic Abilities* (New York: Deepak Chopra Books, 2013), 190.

41. You can download white and pink noise free on the Internet. One good source is http://www.simplynoise.com.

The receiver sits in the chair and puts on the headphones. The two halves of the Ping-Pong ball are placed over his or her eyes. A red light is directed at the receiver's face, creating a pinkish-red effect inside the Ping-Pong ball halves. The receiver keeps his or her eyes open. He or she sits back in the chair, relaxes, and listens to the white or pink noise.

After several minutes, it's common for the receiver to experience hallucinations. He or she then comments on everything he or she experiences for about twenty minutes.

While this is going on, the sender mixes the photographs face-down, and selects four of them without looking at them. The other photographs are put away. The sender turns over one of the four photographs and focuses on it while telepathically sending his or her thoughts about it to the receiver.

Approximately thirty minutes after the experiment began, the white or pink noise is turned off, the Ping-Pong ball halves are removed, and the receiver stands up, stretches, and becomes familiar with his or her surroundings again. He or she is then shown the four selected photographs and asked to rate each one as to how close it was to the thoughts and feelings he or she experienced during the experiment. Finally, the receiver selects the one that most closely matches the thoughts he or she received. The experiment is considered a success if the correct photograph is chosen.

You can make your ganzfeld tests more scientific in a number of ways, especially if you have other people who can help. In this case, the sender and receiver can be in different rooms or even different buildings. If possible, the receiver should be in a soundproof room. Someone other than the sender can choose a selection of, say, eighty photographs and place four of them chosen at random into opaque envelopes. These envelopes are then mixed by a third person, and, someone else, possibly the sender, selects one of them for the experiment. Ideally, the sender should have no communication with the person who chose the photographs until after the experiment, or series of experiments, is over. If possible, everything the receiver says out loud while in the ganzfeld should be recorded for later verification.

A friend named Georgia and I started experimenting with the ganzfeld in the mid-1980s. We used half Ping-Pong balls, static from a radio that was set between two stations, and a table lamp covered with red cellophane. We tossed a coin to see who would be first to try the ganzfeld, and Georgia won.

Once she was resting comfortably in a recliner with half Ping-Pong balls taped to her eyes, I arranged the lamp to provide an even coverage of light over her face, and then I randomly selected four postcards from a selection we had bought especially for the experiment. I mixed these four photographs and again randomly selected one of them. It was a postcard of a beach on a summer's day. People were swimming in the sea and sunbathing on the sand. In the foreground was an old stone building that housed a museum.

It took Georgia longer than I thought it would to fully relax. She kept fidgeting and making grunting noises, though afterward, she told me she'd felt relaxed and wasn't aware of this. At times, it seemed as if she was trying to say something, but she only managed to say letters and partial syllables, rather than complete words. When she stopped moving, I gazed at the postcard and tried to send her impressions of a beautiful beach. I imagined the sound of seagulls and the voices of happy children playing in the sea and on the sand. I tried to transmit the tactile pleasure of walking over warm sand. I visualized the warmth of the sun on my back and the gentle sound of tiny waves lapping on the beach. After a few minutes, I noticed that Georgia wasn't saying anything. We'd agreed that she'd talk about everything she experienced during the exercise.

"Are you receiving anything?" I asked her.

The reply was a giggle.

"Nothing?" I queried.

"It's a dog. I see a dog," Georgia said. "It's beautiful with a long white coat. There's a tiny man sitting on its back, and the dog's running."

I wasn't completely surprised, as I knew she'd probably hallucinate, but I'd imagined bright colors rather than a specific scene.

"Where is it running?"

"I don't know. It's running through a forest full of owls, and they're both laughing." Georgia started giggling. "I'm on the dog's back, too, now, and we're racing up a pink mountain. The little man and I are bouncing up and down on the dog's back."

Georgia stopped talking, and she ignored everything I said for a few minutes. She kept smiling, and because she seemed happy, I wasn't alarmed, even though everything I'd read on the subject suggested that she should keep talking. Finally, I asked, "What's happening now?"

Georgia sighed. "We're on top of the mountain. I don't know where the dog is. The little man is sitting on my shoulder."

"What can you see?"

"I've never seen anything so beautiful before," Georgia said. "The colors are crystal clear and seem to pulsate with energy. I can see for miles and miles all around. This must be an island as I can see beautiful beaches in the distance in every direction, and beyond that the gorgeous blues of the ocean. The vegetation is beyond belief. I can almost watch the plants growing, and they're every color you could possibly imagine. I can hear birds, and the ones I can see are gorgeous, too. The sky is cloudless, and looks like a huge blue canopy that frames everything. It's impossible to describe."

"You're doing well," I said. "What else can you see?"

Georgia hesitated. "Just the colors," she said. "Beautiful, shimmering colors."

She fell silent, and I picked up the photograph and concentrated on it, trying to send her the image of a pleasant summer's day on the beach. Every now and again, Georgia would make a comment about the environment she was in, and how beautiful it all was. She didn't say anything that seemed to relate to the photograph I was gazing at.

After thirty minutes, I said, "It's time to come back now, Georgia. Take a few slow, deep breaths, and I'll take the Ping-Pong balls off your eyes."

I turned off the radio and the red light as she was taking the deep breaths, and then I waited several seconds before removing the Ping-Pong ball halves from her eyes. Georgia looked dazed for about thirty seconds. However, after I gave her some water and a handful of almonds, she returned to normal and told me exactly what happened. At first, she thought it wouldn't work, as all she saw was a blue-green haze, almost as if she was in a fog. That lasted for a long time until she suddenly saw the dog with the little man on it. She wasn't happy when I told her she had to return to her everyday life, and she couldn't believe she'd been in the ganzfeld state for almost thirty minutes.

Finally, I showed her the four photographs. She immediately picked the beach scene that I'd been projecting to her. The other photographs were completely different: A small child watching fireworks, a cruise ship in the middle of the ocean, and a Ford Model T car.

"Why that one?" I asked. She'd said nothing that related to the scene I'd been looking at.

"I could see beaches all around me," Georgia replied. "I didn't see any cruise ships or fireworks. I definitely didn't see any cars, let alone a vintage one."

I wasn't completely convinced, but I had to admit Georgia had picked the right photograph. After that, it was my turn.

I found it easy to relax. For a long time, I "saw" nothing, but all of a sudden I found myself walking along a rain-drenched highway. It had stopped raining, and there was no traffic. It was almost dark. I couldn't see or hear any other signs of life, but it didn't seem strange. It never occurred to me to wonder where I was going. I simply kept walking along the road.

After what seemed like several minutes of walking, I saw a flashing light far ahead. I assumed it was a police car, but when I got closer I saw it was a sign advertising a bar. I walked in and found myself inside what looked like an English pub. There was no one there, but a pint of beer was waiting for me on the bar. I stood at the bar and slowly drank the beer.

When Georgia brought me back to reality, she was extremely excited. She'd been transmitting a picture of three men sitting on a veranda drinking beer. They were obviously in the Deep South, rather than in a pub in England, but beer was definitely involved. When I looked at the four photographs, only one of them involved alcohol or drinks of any sort.

Georgia and I experimented with the ganzfeld for about a year, and then she and her husband moved to another city to further their careers. During that time, we had some amazing successes, but we also had sessions in which nothing happened. We both enjoyed all of the sessions we did together. Although we hallucinated, neither of us experienced the incredible highs that some people report having while in the ganzfeld.

I hope you'll experiment with the ganzfeld. If you talk about the process with friends, you should have no problems finding people willing to participate. It's easy to set up. All you need is a Ping-Pong ball, a source of red light, static sound, and a comfortable chair or bed.

Haragei

Haragei is the Japanese art of communicating thoughts and feelings without the use of words or body language. The thoughts are implied, rather than spoken. Consequently, the silences between the words in a conversation may well be more important or revealing than the spoken words. Japanese business people often utilize haragei when negotiating and in their business dealings. In the West, a silence lasting more than four or five seconds is cause for concern in a conversation, but in a business meeting in Japan no one is bothered if a silence lasts forty seconds or even more.

This concept is sometimes referred to as the "art of the stomach." The word "haragei" comes from *hara*, meaning "belly," and *gei*, which means "sensitivity." In effect, during a conversation between two people, their bellies are talking to each other. Consequently, haragei is sometimes referred to as "belly talk."

In Japan, the belly, or stomach, is sacred, as it is the body's physical and spiritual center and the home of the soul. A "person of hara" is someone who is generous, understanding, compassionate, courageous, confident, and purposeful. He or she possesses great integrity. Someone with a clear conscience is said to have a "clean belly," and someone who "beats the belly drum" leads a happy and contented life.

Belly Talk 1

In this experiment, you and your partner need to stand three or four feet apart, facing each other. Try to keep all expression out of your face, and simply gaze at the other person for five minutes. Do this with gentle eyes. Unlike the eye-gazing experiment you did earlier, you do not need to gaze steadily at the other person's eyes. Allow your eyes to roam anywhere over the other person's face and neck.

Once the five minutes are over, discuss what you experienced during the experiment. Were you thinking similar thoughts? Did you feel a special connection with your partner as you did this? Was it hard or easy to do? Did any special insights about your partner come into your mind as you were gazing at each other?

Belly Talk 2

This test is a more difficult one to arrange, as you need to do it with someone you haven't met. Ideally, you'll meet this person after the experiment. Consequently, you might choose a food court, train or bus station, or anywhere else where you and the other person will be remaining in one place for several minutes. Try to choose someone who looks pleasant and is on his or her own.

As you don't want the person to know you're conducting this experiment, you might like to sit slightly behind and to one side of him or her. Gently gaze at the person for five minutes. It's important that your gaze is kind and nonjudgmental. You don't want the person to become alarmed by the stranger (you) who is staring at him or her.

Wait quietly and see what information comes into your mind about the other person. You may get hints about the person's marital status, number of children, occupation, favorite food, hobbies, interests, and even the type of music he or she likes to listen to. As soon as the five minutes are up, write down everything you've obtained.

The next stage is to find out how accurate you were. Approach the other person and make a comment or ask a question. If you've done this in a food court, you might ask where the person bought his or her meal. In a railway station or airport, you could make a comment about the punctuality of the train or plane you intend catching.

You may find the other person is happy to chat. In that case, you can simply enjoy the conversation and, over a period of time, casually ask questions that relate to what you wrote down. If the other person is reticent, ask him or her an open-ended question. This is a question that can't be answered with a monosyllabic yes or no. You might ask: "Are there other food courts in this area?" If the person says, "Yes," and nothing else, ask how it compares with the one you're currently in. *Is the food better? What makes it better? If that's the case, why are you eating at this one?* Before you know it, you'll be engaged in conversation. Introduce yourself early on in the conversation, and share some information about yourself. This will encourage the other person to tell you something about his or her life, and you'll ultimately find out how good you are at belly talk.

Of course, at this stage, you may or may not tell the other person about your experiment. I prefer not to. This is because not everyone is open-minded about subjects such as mind reading. I've met many interesting people by practicing haragei, and I want them to be left with happy memories of the encounter, rather than worry about what thoughts I'd managed to secretly obtain from them.

In the next chapter, we're going to look at a highly practical form of mind reading. Once you've mastered contact mind reading, you'll be able to demonstrate your skills wherever you happen to be.

Contact mind reading is a subtle process, and it takes practice to master it. Just take your time in learning. With practice you will become an expert in this form of thought communication, and its mastery will increase your sensitivity (awareness) of all you do in life.

—ORMOND MCGILL

chapter 9

CONTACT MIND READING

As its name indicates, contact mind reading involves physical contact between two of the people involved in the experiment. The receiver holds the wrist, or some other part of the sender's body, and picks up thoughts that the sender is thinking about an object or a task he or she wants the receiver to perform. Frequently, the test involves finding an object that has been hidden. The sender knows where it is and telepathically transmits this information step by step to the receiver, who then finds it.

Tests of this sort were regularly used by psychic entertainers in the nineteenth century, and some people still call contact mind reading "Hellstromism" or "Cumberlandism," in recognition of Axel Hellstrom and Stuart Cumberland, who were well known at that time for their contact mind-reading skills. John R. Brown is believed to be the first person to present contact mind reading as an entertainment for the public. He inspired Washington Irving Bishop, who motivated Stuart Cumberland, who in turn inspired others to learn this useful skill.

A number of stage mind readers still present contact mind-reading tests today.

Contact mind reading was also called "muscle reading" by George M. Beard (1839–1883), an American skeptic and neurologist. He thought the sender involuntarily pushed the receiver in the right direction and held him back when he was going in the wrong direction. However, the complexity of experiments that skillful contact mind readers are able to do effectively disproves this explanation. Senders who try to "help" the receiver by pushing or restraining his or her movements cause problems, and they usually have an adverse effect on the demonstration.

Although I have called the two people involved in these experiments the sender and the receiver, you and your partner should take turns in both roles. You should also experiment with as many people as possible playing the role of the sender. You'll find that anyone who is open-minded and curious about mind reading will make a good sender. However, it takes practice to become a good receiver.

How Does It Work?

Contact mind reading works because our bodies all create what is known as the ideomotor response. This is the mechanism that causes a pendulum or divining rod to move. You can even use your entire body as a divining device. If I'm in a bookstore trying to decide which of two books I should buy, I'll place one about a foot to my left and the other approximately a foot to my right. I then close my eyes and ask which of the two books I should buy. My whole body will act as a pendulum and move slightly to indicate the direction of the book that is likely to be more useful to me.

Once you learn to sense another person's ideomotor responses, you'll know that person's thoughts and intentions as they're reflected in unconscious movements made by the body. If you're working on a highly enjoyable hobby or project, you'll probably smile slightly as a physical response to the task you're engaged in. You don't consciously smile because you're having fun. However, your body reflects your feelings of enjoyment. In the same manner, all of your thoughts have a physical effect on your body, and these can be picked up by someone who is attuned to them. When you're holding the hand or wrist of someone, it's possible to pick up the minute unconscious responses the person makes in response to his or her thoughts.

There's an interesting experiment you can try that demonstrates the unconscious responses people make without knowing it. Ask someone to hold out a hand palm up with the fingers spread. Ask him or her to concentrate on one of the fingers. Wait about ten seconds, and then press down on each of the person's fingers one at a time with your forefinger. On one of the fingers you'll feel a greater resistance than on the others, and this will be the finger the person is concentrating on.

The Sender

The sender knows what the outcome of the experiment should be, and he or she simply thinks about the different steps the receiver needs to do to achieve the desired result. He or she doesn't need to make any conscious effort to transmit the thought. However, each thought needs to be made as clearly as possible. Instead of thinking, "I want you to walk to the left-hand corner of the room and touch the third book in the top row of the bookcase," the sender should start by thinking, *Move to the left*. Once the receiver has moved far enough in the desired direction, the sender needs to think, *Stop*, and then think of the next move the receiver has to make. Once he or she is standing in front of the bookcase, the sender needs to think, *Raise your right hand*. When the hand is raised high enough, the sender thinks, *Stop. Now move your hand slowly to the left. Stop. Touch the book directly in front of your hand*. The sender is effectively willing the receiver to perform all the actions he or she focuses on.

When you first start experimenting with this, it may take several minutes for all the thoughts to be transmitted and received. However, with practice you'll find you can achieve apparent miracles in a matter of minutes.

The Receiver

The receiver relaxes and remains alert to any thoughts. If this person feels he or she should "move straight ahead" or "turn left," he or she should immediately act on it. Like the sender, the receiver does not need to make any conscious effort to pick up the thoughts.

I usually stand for a few moments with my eyes closed after I've made physical contact with the sender. I take slow, deep breaths and remain alert to any messages I receive. If I receive nothing, I start to move forward slowly, and almost immediately I'll receive information that I'm going in the right direction or need to turn left or right.

Sometimes a sender will want to guide you in the right direction. This ruins the experiment. To avoid this, you should walk slightly in front of the sender, rather than alongside or behind him or her. Even then, a few people will still try to "help" you. The best way to avoid this problem is to mention it ahead of time and explain how it is actually counterproductive, rather than helpful.

Some receivers find it easier to do contact mind reading when they're blindfolded. This means they're totally reliant on the sender to provide clear mental suggestions on where and when to move to avoid bumping into people, furniture, or breakable objects. Stage performers often use a blindfold, but this is usually done to make the feat appear even more mysterious than it actually is. You might find it helpful to use a blindfold, as it removes the sense of vision. With one sense absent, you'll be able to focus solely on the faint, involuntary impulses that the sender is sending.

Contact

The sender and receiver are in physical contact throughout the experiment. There are many ways of doing this, and you'll have to experiment to see which method works best for you.

1. The most common method is for the receiver to take hold of the sender's wrist using his or her thumb and forefinger. The other fingers rest on the sender's wrist. It makes no difference if the receiver uses his or her left or right hand to hold the sender's wrist.

2. In this method, the sender bends his or her arm at a ninety-degree angle. The receiver puts his or her forearm behind that of the sender and brings his hand up to hold the sender's wrist.

3. This method has the two people making contact with the backs of their hands.

4. The sender and receiver interlock their arms, as if they were two close friends walking along a street.

5. In this method, hold hands with the fingers intertwined. The hands should be held loosely, as too tight a grip makes it harder to feel the vibrations.

6. An unusual method that I've seen only once has the sender making contact with the receiver's forehead with the back of his or her hand.

7. Some people prefer to make contact using a handkerchief or small length of ribbon. The sender holds one end of it, and the receiver holds the other.

8. Instead of a handkerchief, a stick or rod can be used. It should be approximately eighteen to twenty inches long. Both sender and receiver grasp it with their fists.

9. Instead of making contact with the hands, the sender stands behind the receiver and rests his right hand on the receiver's left shoulder.

10. This last method uses both of the receiver's hands. The receiver holds the sender's right wrist with his left hand. His or her right hand also holds the tips of the sender's fingers, with his or her fingers above and thumb below. This is a highly effective clasp, but has the disadvantage that the receiver doesn't have a free hand to reach for the target.

The Chair Test

This is a good experiment to start with. Three chairs are spaced several feet apart from each other. The sender, or someone else, chooses one of them to be the target. Once this has been done, the receiver comes into the room and makes physical contact with the sender. He or she thinks of the first moves the receiver needs to make to end up standing in front of the chosen chair. The receiver should pause, possibly with his or her eyes closed, until he or she feels ready to move.

There's no hurry to perform this initial test. If the receiver hasn't done it before, he or she can use the experience to sense the sender's thoughts and act accordingly. Consequently, he or she might choose to walk up to each chair in turn and see what feelings he or she receives. After this, he or she should know which chair is the target and be able to move directly to it. Once he or she stands in front of the final chair, the receiver should say something along the lines of, "this is it," to confirm his or her choice.

Obviously, the chance score of getting this right is one in three. However, with practice, the receiver should ultimately be able to get it correct every time. Once the receiver is able to do this, the number of chairs can be increased or an additional command can be added to the test. The sender might send a thought instructing the receiver to touch the seat of the chair, sit on it, stand on it, turn it around, or maybe pick it up and move it somewhere else in the room. These additions should not be used until the receiver has gained confidence with his or her contact mind-reading skills.

Finding an Object

The sender goes into a room and chooses something in the room to be the target. Once he or she has done that, the receiver comes into the room and makes physical contact with the sender using one of the methods described above. They both pause for a few moments until the receiver is ready to start. The sender doesn't look at the object, but he or she thinks of the first movements the receiver needs to make to move toward it. This might be, *move straight ahead, walk to the left*, or anything else that will help the receiver move in the right direction. Once the receiver starts moving, the sender telepathically guides him or her until he or she touches the chosen object.

It's easy for the sender to physically guide the receiver by pushing forward or holding back. It's important that he or she doesn't do that, as that defeats the whole object of the exercise. The sender needs to focus his or her attention on the directions, movements, and actions the receiver has to make at each stage of the experiment.

In this example, the receiver successfully locates an object in a room. It's possible for him or her to do the same thing with an object on a tabletop. Here's an interesting experiment to show this.

With the receiver out of the room, the sender chooses six small items from within the room and arranges them on the table. He or she chooses one of the items as the target, and then he or she calls the receiver back in the room. The sender then wills the receiver to move his or her hand across the items. When the receiver's hand is over the chosen item, the sender thinks, *Stop*. If the receiver fails to stop, and he or she continues moving his hand away from the target, the sender thinks, *Go back*, until the receiver does. The receiver might move his hand over the selected item a number of times before he or she realizes that it is the target and drops his or her hand onto it.

Finding a Hidden Object

This test is several steps harder than the preceding ones. In the Finding an Object experiment, the receiver had to locate an object that was in plain sight in the room. In this experiment, he or she has to find an object that has been hidden from view. In time, the receiver will be able to find objects as small as a pin, but initially the object should be at least the size of a ballpoint pen.

The sender hides the object somewhere in the room. He or she might place it in a drawer or a cupboard, hide it behind a curtain or a picture, or place it under a chair or a sofa. The important thing is that it needs to be hidden somewhere the receiver will be able to reach it without needing a ladder or a chair and without causing damage to the room.

Once the object has been hidden from view, the receiver comes in. After physical contact has been made, the sender thinks of the first actions he or she needs to do. This will successfully guide him or her to the area where the object is hidden. The sender now has to lead him or her to the exact place where it is concealed. He or she must mentally tell the receiver to raise or lower a hand, kneel, open a cupboard or a drawer, or do whatever else is necessary until the object is found.

It's perfectly acceptable for the receiver to talk during this, or any, test. Some people keep up a running commentary all the way through the experiment, some talk only when necessary, and others don't talk at all. The receiver might, for instance, say to the sender: "I'm completely at a loss. Please think left or right... That's good, I'll move to the right... Oh, I sense you want me to go back. I must have gone too far. This feels better. I think you and I will be able to do this. I think you want me to look lower. I'm bending down. I can't sense anything—yes, I can, you're telling me to look under the chair. I still can't see it, ah, here it is!"

Once the receiver has gained skill at this, the scope can be widened considerably. The object could be hidden somewhere in an entire house or even in a large office building. In fact, there is no limit—even if it is hidden somewhere in a large city, as long as the sender knows where it is hidden, he or she could transmit the necessary information to the receiver and guide him or her to it.

Finding a Person

You can conduct any of these experiments in a social setting. People enjoy watching them, and they will be impressed with your new-found skill. Although these tests can be presented in a light-hearted way, your guests must be told beforehand not to help or hinder the receiver, as this is likely to ruin the demonstration.

In this test, one person in a group is chosen to be the target. The receiver has to find this person and shake his or her hand. Once the receiver and sender have made physical contact, the receiver moves according to the thoughts he or she receives until he or she has shaken hands with the target person.

Again, there's no limit to the number of people who can be involved in the experiment. Once you're able to do it in a room full of people, there's no reason why you can't do it successfully in a large stadium filled with tens of thousands of people.

Finding a Playing Card

A deck of cards is thoroughly shuffled and the cards are spread out on a table. While the receiver is out of the room, the spectators choose one of the cards as the target. The receiver returns and takes the sender's hand, moving it to and fro across the table. Once the receiver senses he is in the right area, he moves the hand in decreasing circles until he feels he is over the correct card. He then lowers his hand to the card, picks it up, and shows it to the audience.

Finding a Playing Card Variation

In this test, one of the spectators chooses a card from a shuffled deck, shows it to the audience, and returns it to the deck. The cards are shuffled again, and the deck is placed faceup on a table. The receiver, who was out of the room while the card was selected, returns. He or she takes hold of the sender's hand, and with his or her free hand picks up the cards one at a time. Each card is held briefly in his or her hand before being placed to one side. The receiver continues doing this until sensing that he or she is holding the correct card.

This test is more difficult than the first demonstration of finding a playing card. It is worth persevering with though, as once you can do it successfully, you can make it even more impressive by having the audience choose a particular poker hand, such as two pairs, three of a kind, or a royal flush. This demonstration looks more and more impossible as you detect the correct cards one at a time.

Locating a Book

This test is similar to finding a person, except a book is located in a bookcase, or even in a bookstore or library. Once the receiver has gained sufficient experience, he or she will be able to take the correct book out of the bookcase and open it to a specific page that the sender is sending to him. If desired, the receiver can even locate a single word on the chosen page that the sender is thinking of. This is an advanced experiment, but one that can be achieved with practice.

Horoscope Sign

Almost everyone knows their horoscope sign, and you can easily divine this information using contact mind reading. All you need is a large piece of cardboard with the twelve signs of the zodiac written on it. Anyone who wants to test the receiver whispers his or her sign to the sender. The receiver passes his free hand over each sign in turn while the sender thinks about what the receiver should do next. He or she might think: *Keep going ... Farther ... farther ... almost there ... stop now.* If the receiver fails to pick up the sign and continues moving his hand farther away from the person's sign, the sender might think: *Stop. Go back. More ... a bit more, and stop now.*

This is a popular test, and if you present this for a group of people, you'll find everyone will want to see if you can locate his or her zodiac sign.

If you wish, you can expand this test to include the person's day and month of birth. To do this, write down the months and the numbers from one to thirty-one on a sheet of cardboard, and divine the month followed by the day.

Whodunnit?

As your skills at contact mind reading develop, you'll be able to create entertaining scenarios that your guests will enjoy. Washington Irving Bishop was aware that his acts needed to be entertaining, and he regularly performed a murder mystery as part of his show in the 1870s and 1880s. The murder mystery still entertains audiences today.

You (the receiver) play the part of the detective. While you're out of the room, one of your guests is chosen to be the murderer and someone else is selected to be the victim.

When you return to the room, the sender will think about the necessary steps you need to make to locate first the victim and then the murderer. If you wish, you can expand this test by using another person who is concealing the murder weapon, and someone else who is holding a valuable clue. In this case, you'd start by finding the victim, followed by the murder weapon, the clue, and finally the murderer.

Instead of a murder theme, you might be the detective who arrests a jewel thief, finds the jewels, and returns them to their rightful owner.

Tests of this sort are always well received, and your guests will have a great deal to think about long after the demonstration has taken place.

Telepathic Postman

In this experiment, the receiver delivers an envelope to the right person. This is an entertaining test for a group of people, and it's made even more special if the message inside the envelope has a particular meaning for the recipient. On one occasion, someone at a party I attended was given an envelope containing a birthday card, as it happened to be her birthday. On another occasion, I saw someone presented with an envelope containing a message saying that he was "employee of the month." It's wonderful when the test can be personalized like this, but it's just as impressive to deliver an envelope to the right person in a room containing twenty or more people.

Hidden Ring

In this test, a borrowed ring is hidden somewhere in the room. The receiver is able to find the ring, locate its owner, and place the ring back on the correct finger.

Brooch or Necklace Effect

This is an entertaining experiment that can be presented at any social event. While the receiver is out of the room, one of the women present removes a brooch, necklace, or piece of jewelry. This item is placed on another woman in a different part of the room. When the receiver returns, he or she has to find the item, remove it, and then return it to its owner, placing it back in its correct position.

Rings on Her Fingers

While the receiver is out of the room, a lady in the audience removes a ring and gives it to the sender. The receiver returns and is handed the ring. He or she proceeds to find the lady and replaces the ring on the correct finger. In this experiment the sender needs to see which finger the ring came from so the receiver can return it correctly.

Husband and Wife

Three men and three women are selected to act as three couples while the receiver is out of the room. It's more fun if the men and women do not already know each other. The receiver has to identify all six people and then arrange them into couples.

Writing a Chosen Word

This test is not as entertaining as some of the earlier ones, but it still makes an impressive demonstration. You'll need a large piece of cardboard with all the letters of the alphabet written on it. The sender thinks of any word in the English language. As the sender thinks of it, one letter at a time, the receiver passes his or her free hand over each letter in turn. Each time he or she "finds" a letter, it is written down until the entire word has been spelled out, one letter at a time.

A less time-consuming experiment can be done using telephone numbers instead of words. In this case all the numbers from zero to nine are written down, and the receiver divines the numbers one by one until the full telephone number has been revealed.

The same chart of numbers can be used to determine the page number of a chosen book, the day and month of a particular event, the time of day a particular event occurred, and even the serial numbers on a dollar bill.

Drawing Test

The sender thinks of a geometric shape and the receiver draws it on a whiteboard or a sheet of paper. It's best to start with simple designs, such as a square, circle, or triangle. However, with practice, it's possible to receive a great deal more than this. Complicated pictures can be sent, especially when the sender is able to see it while sending the necessary information.

The number of tests that can be performed with contact mind reading is virtually limitless, and a number of entertainers have used their ability at this to create successful careers for themselves. In fact, the first time I saw contact mind reading presented was in the early 1970s, when I saw well-known psychic entertainer Kreskin find the paycheck for his performance in the inside pocket of a man's suit in a packed theatre. Obviously, there is more pressure put on the performer when his paycheck is at stake, but in reality, this test is no more difficult than the other experiments described in this chapter.

Contact mind reading is usually performed before an audience. However, these people are observers, rather than participants, in the experiments. In the next chapter, we'll look at a number of experiments that are done with, rather than for, groups of people.

The phenomenon of spontaneous telepathic accord is frequently realized in spirit séances, in churches, concert halls, theaters, conferences, public gatherings, and between two persons living together in the same house, and in the same locality, in the same country. It is possible to state the phenomenon thus: When several persons perceive the same object, there may be telepathic accord among them. As a corollary: When several participants think together of the same agent, they may be in telepathic accord themselves.

—RENÉ WARCOLLIER

chapter 10

GROUP TESTS

If you are fortunate enough to know a large number of people who are interested in psychic matters, you can conduct some large-scale experiments.

A good example of an experiment of this sort was conducted by Guy Lyon Playfair, the well-known author and psychic investigator, who conducted an experiment with an audience of eighty-five people in August 1981. He tuned a radio to an unused frequency to fill the room with white noise. He then told the audience to relax, and even go to sleep, if they wished. Once everyone was sufficiently relaxed, Playfair randomly chose one postcard from a group of four, went behind a screen, and tried to transmit the picture he was looking at to the audience. The postcard showed a picture of Chatsworth House.

Playfair concentrated on the picture while mentally repeating the words, *castle, bridge, river, trees* over and over again. He also visualized the castle, bridge, river, and trees filling up the room the experiment was being conducted in.

Once he'd done that, Playfair passed the four postcards around the audience and asked them to decide which one he had attempted to transmit to them. Thirty-five percent correctly picked Chatsworth House. However, another 25 percent chose a painting of a Flemish castle surrounded by trees. The other two postcards received 10 and 12 percent of the votes, respectively.[42]

A Few Friends

You will need to involve a few friends for this experiment. For the sake of explanation, I'll assume that you'll be the receiver. You and your friends need to decide on a particular time to perform the experiment. Your friends also need to decide which one of them will send you a thought at that particular time.

A few minutes before the designated time, you need to sit or lie down, close your eyes, and relax as much as possible. Once you feel totally relaxed, allow your mind to drift as you wait for the thought to come through. Remain in this relaxed state for at least ten minutes. This ensures that the person sending you the thought has a little bit of leeway in time, just in case he or she might be delayed by a phone call or some other interruption.

Once you get up, write down everything you can think of that popped into your mind while you were relaxed and receptive. In addition to this, you need to ascertain which of your friends sent you the thought. Once you've done this, call this person to verify your accuracy.

Hopefully, you'll have contacted the right person and also picked up the thought. However, you might have contacted the right person

---

42. Guy Lyon Playfair, *If This Be Magic: The Forgotten Power of Hypnosis* (London: Jonathan Cape Limited, 1985), 116–118.

but failed to pick up the thought. You might have called the wrong person but picked up the thought that another friend sent to you. In a worst-case scenario, you'll have contacted the wrong person and failed to pick up the thought.

You'll find your accuracy will increase with practice. You and your friends should take turns as senders and receivers. You'll find that some people are better at knowing who sent the thought than they are at picking up the thought, while others might be good at catching the thought, but they find it harder to determine who sent it.

Same or Different

The purpose of this experiment is to see if two people can tell if someone else is looking at the same photograph as they are at the exact same time. You'll need two each of at least twenty photographs. The photographs are split into two decks, each containing a complete set of twenty photographs. Each deck is thoroughly mixed.

Two people are placed back to back, and they are each given one of the decks facedown. When the timekeeper tells them to start, they each turn over the top photograph and stare at it for ten seconds. After this, the timekeeper asks them if they thought the other person was looking at the same photograph as they were. If desired, the time-keeper can give immediate feedback on the result. Alternatively, the results can be given at the end of the run of photographs. After this the timekeeper tells them to turn over the next photo. This process is continued until all the photographs in the deck have been looked at.

It's important that the timekeeper doesn't look at the photographs, at least until after asking the question. This is to prevent the participants from inadvertently picking up the timekeeper's thoughts. It's important to ensure that the only people being tested are the two people holding the cards.

As both decks of photographs have been thoroughly mixed before-hand, it's possible that none of the photographs will match.

Ten to Ninety-Nine

Every person in a group is given a drawing pad and a marker. They all sit facing in the same direction. One person is chosen to be the sender. This person sits behind everyone else and writes a two-digit number on his or her drawing pad. He or she concentrates on the two digits he or she has drawn and tries to transmit it to the rest of the group. The receivers write down the numbers they receive, and the results are compared.

With one receiver, the odds are one in ninety. The odds for success in this experiment are determined by dividing ninety by the number of receivers in the particular test. I personally find this test extremely difficult, as numbers lack emotion, and this makes them hard to pick up.

The Power of Emotions

You'll need to collect about two dozen photographs of emotionally charged events for this test. Half of these should illustrate positive emotions, such as two lovers gazing into each other's eyes. The other half should contain negative emotions, such as two people arguing. The photographs are placed into opaque envelopes and mixed thoroughly.

You can perform this experiment with as many people as you wish. It can be done with as little as two people, a sender and a receiver. However, you can have as many senders and receivers as you wish. Let's assume you have four senders and four receivers.

The receivers go to another room and wait for the thought to arrive. Once they are out of sight and hearing, one of the envelopes is chosen and the senders concentrate on the emotion that the photograph reveals.

The receivers' task is to pick up the emotion and decide if it is positive or negative. Each receiver should write down his or her thought before discussing anything with the other receivers. They then return to the room the senders are in to check their results.

Obviously, the odds are fifty-fifty in this experiment. Consequently, it needs to be repeated a number of times to demonstrate telepathic ability. You might like to have a run of, say, ten experiments, followed by a brief break for refreshments and to move around. After that, everyone changes roles, and another run of ten is made.

This experiment is similar to a Swedish study on telepathically communicating emotions conducted in 1998.[43]

The Wiseman Experiment

In December 2000, Dr. Richard Wiseman, the eminent UK psychologist and author, conducted an experiment that involved up to one hundred people. The person chosen to be the receiver sat in one room of a university building. In another room in the same building, fifty to one hundred people were shown a picture. They all had to concentrate on sending this image to the receiver.

After this, the receiver was shown four pictures and asked to decide which of them had been transmitted. Unfortunately, the results proved inconclusive. All the same, this is an intriguing experiment to replicate if you have access to a large number of people who are willing to participate.

Party Games

Group tests are often used as party games. Two well-known examples of these are the Willing Game and the Guessing Game. Ideally, these should be conducted at a reasonably fast pace to give everyone the opportunity to be the psychic. They should also be done in a light-hearted manner, as they are often presented as after-dinner entertainment. Many people believe that the best results come when there is little pressure on the psychic to succeed.

43. Jan Dalkvist and Joakim Westerlund, "Experimental Studies on Telepathic Group Communication of Emotions," *Journal of Scientific Exploration* 12 *(No. 4,* 1998): 583–603, http://www.scientificexploration.org/journal/jse_12_4_dalkvist.pdf.

The Willing Game

Someone is chosen to be the receiver. He or she is escorted outside a room while the people remaining inside jointly choose an object that the receiver has to pick up and hold. When the receiver returns to the room, everyone has to concentrate on the object and "will" the receiver to it. As well as thinking about the object, they all have to actively "will" the receiver to move in the right directions and ultimately pick up the object. It's important that none of the people in the room stare at the chosen object or make any comments about whether the receiver is "hot or cold."

This is not contact mind reading, as there is no physical contact between the receiver and anyone else. All he or she has to go on are the thoughts of all the people in the room. The receiver needs to remain completely passive and move in the direction that the other participants are willing him or her to make.

The Guessing Game

As in the Willing Game, the person selected to be the receiver is escorted from the room. The people inside the room decide on any object inside the room. When the receiver returns, the group focuses on the object. The receiver needs to remain relaxed and passive, and he or she must wait for the name or feeling about the object to come into his or her mind. The key to success is for the receiver to say the name of the first object that comes into his or her mind. If he or she thinks about whether or not the thought is correct, the experiment is likely to end in failure.

Once the receiver gains experience at naming objects in the room, the committee can start thinking of any object they care to name.

These experiments should also be done with the receiver outside the room, as it's possible that one of the people inside the room may inadvertently provide clues about the selected object.

The Sway Test

You'll need five people for this test. One person is designated the receiver, and he or she goes to another room. The remaining four decide on a direction—forward, backward, to the left, or to the right. Once this has been decided, the receiver comes back into the room. He or she stands up straight, with feet together and head facing directly ahead. The other four people circle him or her. One stands directly in front, another directly behind, and the other two on either side. These four people all place their hands gently on the receiver's shoulders.

The receiver closes his or her eyes, and the other four people concentrate on the direction they want the person to sway toward. They should all visualize the receiver doing this.

The receiver needs to relax and allow him- or herself to sway in whatever direction he or she senses is right. The other four people need to be ready to prevent the receiver from falling over if he or she sways too far.

This experiment should be repeated until the receiver succeeds. Once this happens, someone else takes a turn at being the receiver, and the process is continued until everyone has had a turn.

Here's Looking at You, Kid

Since 1995, the Science Centre NEMO, a science museum in Amsterdam, has been conducting an interesting experiment based on the pioneering work of the renowned English scientist Dr. Rupert Sheldrake. It involves *The Sense of Being Stared At*, which happens to be the title of one of his many books.

In the science museum, the experiment is conducted in a room that is empty except for two chairs, one in front of the other, and a computer screen that has been placed between them. Volunteers sit in the two chairs. A message appears on the computer screen telling the person in the back chair whether or not to stare at the back of the head of the person sitting in front of him or her. If the computer tells him or her to stare at the other person, he or she does this for thirty seconds. The person in front then has to say whether or not the other person is staring at him or her. The person in the back chair enters whatever occurs into the computer.

This experiment is conducted thirty times. After that, these two people leave the room, and another two people take their places. Between 1995 and 2002, almost 19,000 pairs of people tried this experiment. The results were incredible. People have been correct so often that the chances of the results occurring simply by chance are 10 to the power of 376. That is a 1 followed by 72 zeros![44]

You can replicate this test if you're in a position to work with a group of people. Instead of a computer, you could use a third person to indicate whether or not the person should stare at the person in front of him or her. Another person could also record the findings.

In his book, *Seven Experiments That Could Change the World*, Dr. Sheldrake suggests a highly practical way of performing this test. He proposes that the person who does the staring tosses a coin to determine whether or not he or she should stare or look away. Heads could mean "stare" and tails "look away." This person can make a tapping or clicking sound to indicate the start of each trial. About ten seconds after hearing the tapping sound, the person should say whether or not he or she is being stared at. This experiment can be performed with or without immediate feedback. Dr. Sheldrake feels both versions provide positive results, but he prefers immediate feedback, as this makes the experiment more interesting for the two people involved.

Dr. Sheldrake also says that twenty seconds is long enough for each test and that experiments should last approximately twenty minutes,

44. Jeremy Smith, "Telepathy: A New Way of Seeing," *The Ecologist* (September 1, 2005), http://www.theecologist.org/investigations/society/268826/telepathy_a_new_way_of_seeing.html.

which provides enough time for forty tests. For statistical purposes, he recommends repeating the experiment on ten different occasions.[45]

If some of the people are in permanent relationships, you could test to see if they produced better or worse results when doing this experiment with their partner, than they did with acquaintances or total strangers.

The Noncontact Touch Experiment

As its name indicates, this experiment is similar to contact mind reading, but without the contact. It can be done with any number of people. Ideally, you'll need about ten people to provide useful results. The receiver leaves the room, and the remaining people decide which person they'll telepathically ask him or her to touch.

When the receiver returns, the group forms a circle around him or her and mentally directs the receiver to the correct person. This is done in stages. They may all think, *Turn around*, *Move forward*, or *Stop* for instance. They continue sending the receiver mental directions until he or she finds the right person and reaches out to touch him or her.

The receiver must remain as relaxed as possible and respond to any impressions that come into his or her mind. If you are the receiver, you may feel pressure to move as everyone will be observing everything you do. Resist this. Take as much time as necessary, and do whatever is necessary each time you feel an impulse.

The people sending the information need to make sure they don't inadvertently help the sender with their facial expressions or by staring at the target person.

An Evening at Home

This is an enjoyable experiment that you can try with a group of friends. While you're out of the room, each of your friends needs to

45. Rupert Sheldrake, *Seven Experiments That Could Change the World: A Do-It-Yourself Guide to Revolutionary Science* (New York: Riverhead, 1995), 113–115.

perform a simple action. One might stand in front of the fireplace, another could sit down and read a newspaper, a third might write a letter, and two others may enjoy a conversation. Your friends perform whatever task they've chosen for five minutes. They then change positions and invite you back into the room.

You may have picked up some thoughts during the five minutes your friends were acting out their tasks. If so, you can start talking about them first. If not, look around the room and see what comes into your mind. You might, for instance, say that John was standing by the fireplace, which is correct. You may then say that Bill was sitting at the table. This is also partially correct, as Bill was writing a letter while seated at the table. In this case, your friends should tell you what Bill was doing, as this could help you gain further insights into what everyone was doing.

Once you've told your friends everything that appeared in your mind, someone else takes a turn outside the room, and the experiment is repeated.

An interesting alternative to this is for the person who is outside the room to write down all the impressions that come to him or her before coming into the room.

Acting Out Your Emotions

This test works well as a follow-up to the experiment An Evening at Home. The group starts by creating a list of common emotions. These could include anger, disgust, fear, happiness, and sadness. The receiver leaves the room, and the senders decide on the particular emotion they plan to transmit. Once they've made a choice, they act out a scene that incorporates the selected emotion. If, for instance, anger is the chosen emotion, the senders could form two groups of people who are extremely angry at each other. If happiness is chosen, they could act out being especially happy with the success of a colleague.

Once they have completed this reenactment, everyone sits down and puts on a neutral expression. The receiver is brought into the room and has to sense the emotion and what the senders did to create it.

Frequently, the receiver will already know the emotion, as he or she will have picked it up while the scene was being acted out. On other occasions, he or she will need to sense the emotions in the room and say what he or she thinks it is.

This is an enjoyable experiment that works well if it's done quickly and everyone has a turn.

It's one thing to send a thought to another human being and to receive a thought back in return. It's quite another to exchange thoughts with an animal. This is not as strange as it may sound, and many people communicate with their pets regularly using mind-to-mind communication. We'll discuss this fascinating aspect of mind reading in the next chapter.

Sigh like the wind—open your arms, your chest,
your heart—and all creatures will hum to you.
—PENELOPE SMITH

chapter 11

INTERSPECIES
COMMUNICATION

In a lecture called "Biology and Telepathy" that he presented at Aberdeen University in 1963, Professor Sir Alister Hardy (1896–1985), the distinguished biologist and Fellow of the Royal Society, said: "If it [mind reading] is proved in man, and I believe the evidence is overwhelming, and if we believe that man is one with the stream of life, then it seems that it is most unlikely that so remarkable a phenomenon should be confined to just a few individuals of just one species of animal."

In his lecture, Sir Alister hypothesized that there could be "a general subconscious sharing of form and behavior pattern—a sort of psychic 'blueprint'—shared between members of a species." [46] In this chapter, we'll take Sir Alister's belief a step further by discussing mind reading between humans and animals.

---

46. The series of Gifford Lectures that Sir Alister Hardy presented at Aberdeen University were later published in two volumes, *The Living Stream* and *The Divine Flame*. "Biology and Telepathy" was included as Chapter Nine in: Sir Alister Hardy, *The Living Stream: Evolution and Man* (London: William Collins, 1965).

In the late 1990s, Dr. Rupert Sheldrake conducted a survey of pet owners. He found that 48 percent of dog owners and 33 percent of cat owners believed their pets could telepathically respond to their thoughts.[47] This shows that many people have had the experience of communicating telepathically with their pet.

Even people who say they have never communicated telepathically with their pets may, in fact, have done so unwittingly. Many cat and dog owners, for instance, have had the experience of their pet disappearing shortly before they were planning to take it to the vet or give it a bath. Many animals seem to know when their owners are going to go out and leave them behind. This often occurs well before the owner has made any physical indication of leaving. These are examples of the pet picking up the unspoken thoughts of its owner.

Dogs, in particular, seem to be extremely good at anticipating walks. In his book, *Kinship with All Life*, J. Allen Boone (1882–1965) told how he was working at his desk one day while Strongheart, the German shepherd dog he was looking after, was in another room. Strongheart (1917–1929) was a remarkable animal. He was a former police dog in Germany who came to the United States at the age of three and played a starring role in several Hollywood movies in the 1920s.

Boone didn't feel like working, and he thought how wonderful it would be to take Strongheart for a walk in the hills. While he was still thinking about this, Strongheart bounded into his office in a state of great excitement. He licked Boone's hand, and then he brought out Boone's sweater, jeans, boots, and walking stick, one at a time. As Boone had not said a single word out loud about taking a walk, Strongheart had obviously read his mind.[48] Needless to say, Boone gave up all thoughts of working and spent the rest of the day in the hills with Strongheart.

---

47. David Jay Brown and Rupert Sheldrake, "Perceptive Pets: A Survey in North-West California," *Journal of the Society for Psychical Research* 62 (July 1998): 396–406, http://www.sheldrake.org/Articles&Papers/papers/animals/perceptivecalif.html.
48. J. Allen Boone, *Kinship with All Life* (New York: Harper & Row, 1954), 35.

Barbara Woodhouse (1910–1988), the famous British dog trainer, considered telepathy a vital part of her training methods. In her book, *No Bad Dogs: The Woodhouse Way*, she wrote: "Above all, you need telepathy so that the dog thinks with you." [49]

Interspecies telepathic communication is not restricted to humans and dogs. Whether you are aware of it or not, you are constantly sending messages to your pet.

When Eden, my oldest granddaughter, was a preschooler, she used to enjoy playing with our rabbit, Tibbar (rabbit spelled backward). Tibbar appeared to enjoy being dressed in doll clothes and taken for rides in a baby carriage. However, whenever Eden thought it was time to put him back in his cage he'd hide under her bed and refuse to let her catch him.

We used to have a cat called Killy. As she grew older, she spent more and more time sleeping in different hiding places that she found. We could search the house calling for her, and she wouldn't respond. However, as soon as we thought about feeding her, she'd instantly appear.

In her book *Pets Have Souls Too*, Jenny Smedley tells the story of a woman called Mimi Lawrence and Joey, her pet tortoise. She noticed that whenever she went to feed Joey, he'd be waiting for her at his feeding tray. When she mentioned this to her husband, he laughed and said it was obviously because Joey could hear her coming or possibly because she fed him at the same time every day. Mimi decided to experiment by feeding Joey at different times of the day. Somehow, no matter what time it was, he'd be at the tray waiting for her. However, whenever she asked her husband to feed him, Joey wouldn't be there. Mimi was delighted to have evidence that Joey was reading her mind. [50]

Dr. J. B. Rhine was particularly fascinated with the psychic bond between a young boy called Hugh Perkins, from West Virginia, and his

---

49. Barbara Woodhouse, *No Bad Dogs: The Woodhouse Way* (New York: Simon & Schuster, 1984), http://www.goodreads.com/author/quotes/241134.Barbara _Woodhouse.

50. Jenny Smedley, *Pets Have Souls Too* (Carlsbad, CA: Hay House, 2009), 116–117.

pet pigeon. The pigeon arrived unexpectedly in Hugh's backyard and, despite having an identifying band around one leg, it showed no interest in leaving. Hugh started feeding it, and during the following twelve months the boy and pigeon developed a close bond.

About a year later, Hugh became ill and was rushed to a hospital 120 miles away for an operation. The following night, there was a gentle tapping at the window of Hugh's room. Hugh could see a pigeon standing on the window ledge, but he was not well enough to get out of bed and let it in. The bird stayed there all night in the winter snow until a nurse opened the window in the morning.[51]

Dr. Rupert Sheldrake reported a fascinating case in which telepathic communication between a woman and her dog saved her life. The woman, who lived in the north of England, was suffering major marital problems and decided to end her life. Her dog and cats were sleeping in front of the fire when she went out to the kitchen for Paracetamol and water. Suddenly, William, her fifteen-year-old springer spaniel, raced up to her and snarled. He had never done this before. The dog's "jowls were pulled completely back so that he was almost unrecognizable." The woman was terrified. She immediately replaced the lid on the bottle of tablets and returned to the sofa in the living room. William followed her back and licked her face frantically, his whole body wagged in happiness.[52]

The first scientific experiments involving interspecies communication between humans and dogs were in Russia. Vladimir M. Bekhterev and Alexander Leontovich, two Soviet academicians, gave Vladimir Durov (1863–1934), an experienced animal trainer, a note containing instructions for a test they wanted Mars, a German shepherd that was famous in Russia for his ability to count and dance, to attempt. After

---

51. Joseph E. Wylder, *Psychic Pets* (New York: Stonehill Publishing Company, 1978), 66. This story is also included in *Into the Unknown* (Sydney, Australia: Readers Digest Services, 1982), 242–244.

52. Rupert Sheldrake, *Dogs That Know When Their Owners Are Coming Home and Other Unexplained Powers of Animals* (London: Hutchinson and Company, 1999), 77.

reading the note, Durov held the dog's head between the palms of his hands and gazed into his eyes. When he let go, Mars did nothing. Durov gazed into Mars's eyes again, and this time Mars went into a room he had never been in before. The room contained three tables full of files. Mars stood on his hind legs to examine the objects on the first table. He did this again with the second table. On the third table he found what he was looking for. He grabbed the phone book with his mouth and took it back to Durov. This was exactly what the scientists had written on the note, and Durov had successfully transmitted the instructions to Mars using telepathy.[53]

After this impressive start, the academicians devised a series of tests that Mars and a Scottish terrier named Pikki performed perfectly. Vladimir Durov, who'd started his career as a circus acrobat, became director of the Zoopsychological Laboratory in Moscow, where he continued his telepathy experiments until his death in 1934. He wrote a book called *Training of Animals* that taught his methods of communicating telepathically with dogs.

Durov believed the most important factor in telepathic communication between the trainer and the dog was a close emotional bond. Before each test, it was important to attract and hold the dog's attention. Durov did this by holding the dog's head in his hands and staring into the dog's eyes. He then visualized the dog doing all the required actions to complete the test, and he focused on sending that message to the dog. The dog was rewarded with a piece of fresh meat after each successful test.

If you have a pet, you can send it telepathic messages and see what response you receive in return. The best results occur when you are both free from stress. Start by playing a game or giving your pet a hug. After you've been playing for a while, think of something that relates to you and your pet. A simple message saying how much you love it

---

53. Sheila Ostrander and Lynn Schroeder, *Psychic Discoveries Behind the Iron Curtain* (Englewood Cliffs, NJ: Prentice-Hall, Inc, 1970), 132–134.

is usually sufficient. Even though the game or hug is still in progress, you'll be able to tell from the look on your pet's face that it has picked up the thought. You may receive an instant answer to your message. Once you've finished the hug or game, sit down and relax. Your pet might want further attention, but it will quickly see that the petting is over.

Wait for about a minute, and then send a telepathic message to your pet. Express your appreciation and love. Tell your pet how much you love it and what the relationship means to you. You may find it helpful to send thoughts in pictures. Visualize yourself stroking and petting your pet while observing what he or she does. When you've finished, sit quietly and see what comes into your mind. You may find your pet sending similar thoughts back to you. You may receive a comforting sense that your pet loves you. If you're fortunate, you may receive a message. It's important to communicate with your pet as if you were talking to a close friend. After all, this is what you are doing.

If you regularly communicate telepathically with your pet, you'll find your relationship becoming closer and closer, and you'll be able to exchange thoughts, ideas, and feelings. It takes practice. Be patient; allow as much time as necessary for this special bond to develop.

Some people are naturally good at interspecies communication. With other people it takes time and practice. I think it's a skill that anyone can develop, as most pet owners instinctively know if their pet is feeling happy, scared, bored, or unwell. Interspecies communication is only one small step beyond that.

People who haven't tried this sometimes think that it's impossible, as animals don't understand many words. Obviously, your pet will know its name, as well as words that relate to its needs. However, it also knows a surprising number of other words, as you'll discover when you start communicating telepathically with it.

Cats are a good example. In addition to words such as "dinner," "beautiful, and "play," the average cat understands more than one hundred common words.[54] I believe that cats can also pick up the pictures we create in our minds.

When you communicate with your pet, you should always talk in terms of what you'd like it to do, rather than what you want it to avoid. If you want to telepathically tell your dog to stop digging holes in the garden, for instance, you shouldn't say, "Don't do that." Instead, you should talk in terms of what you want. You might mentally send a message to your dog saying something along the lines of: "I've worked long and hard on the garden to make it look nice and attractive. I like looking at it, and want it to remain looking beautiful for when friends come to visit. I know the garden is soft and nice to dig in, but I'd really like it if you could dig holes somewhere else. Would you please help me by doing that?"

Of course, there'll be times when your pet won't want to listen to requests of this sort. This is especially the case if it walks away while you're sending the thought. If your pet doesn't want to listen, you need to repeat it while making direct eye contact. Hold your pet's head and gaze into its eyes. Explain that you wouldn't be making this request if it wasn't important to you. Repeat the request and ask your pet to respond. It might take your pet several seconds to respond, as it will be thinking about your request. The response might appear as thoughts in your mind, or you may receive a friendly lick on your hand or face. Once your pet has given a positive reply, you'll know that it will follow it most of the time.

It's important to receive a positive response. If you don't, your pet will feel free to ignore your request, especially if you're asking it to stop doing something it finds enjoyable. Consequently, you need to wait a short while, and then make the same request again, and again if need be, until you receive a positive answer.

---

54. Milton Kreutzer, quoted in Jhan Robbins, *Your Pet's Secret Language* (New York: Warner Books, 1975), 123.

You may want to give your pet a reward when it accedes to your requests. This doesn't necessarily mean food. A play in the park, time with its friends, or an extra-long walk are all good ways to reward your pet.

Naturally, you must praise your pet when it does something right. Continue thanking your pet for its new behavior as frequently as possible.

It's all very well to send telepathic messages to your pet, but you must also listen to what it has to say. People are often told, "You never listen." This is the case when animals send messages, too. You need to remain receptive to your pet's messages to you. A good way to practice this is to remain alert to any thoughts or feelings that occur to you while you're stroking or cuddling your pet. They can appear as thoughts, pictures, or ideas. There'll be times when you may not realize that the thought has come from your pet. However, there'll be many other times when the thought could not have come from anyone else.

It's important to remain impartial and accepting of these thoughts. If you react badly or become emotional, your pet might choose to stop communicating with you.

You and your pet don't need to be together to communicate telepathically. If your pet is not with you, picture it in your mind, and mentally repeat its name. This will attract your pet's attention, no matter where it might be. Once you've done this, you can send it thoughts and messages wherever you happen to be and receive messages in return. This can be especially useful if you are parted from your pet for any length of time. A friend of mine in the United Kingdom, who travels regularly on business, sends loving thoughts to his cat and dog every day when he's away, and he receives responses from them.

It's best to start practicing psychic communication with your own pet, at least initially. Once you've become proficient at this, you can start experimenting with other animals. If the animal you're trying to communicate with has been abused or injured, you should start by surrounding him or her with a healing light. I mentally surround the animal with a clear white light, but I know several people who prefer to surround animals with a rainbow of light.

Ask the animal what you can do to make his or her life better. Listen and act upon whatever it is you're told.

Like anything else, it takes time to develop your skills at communicating with pets and other animals. Practice wherever you happen to be and whenever you can.

When I first started experimenting with this, a good friend gave me some valuable advice. She told me to relax and have fun with it. "It doesn't work if you're anxious or stressed. Relax, and simply allow it to happen."

Remote Experiment

This is a simple experiment that often provides surprising results. Ask someone to look after your pet while you're away from home. At a mutually agreed upon time, start thinking about your pet and talk to it in your mind. Close your eyes for a few seconds and imagine you're stroking it.

When you return home, ask the person who was minding your pet if it did anything unusual or different at the time you were transmitting thoughts to it. If your pet responded well, you can repeat the experiment, but this time don't tell your sitter the time when you'll be sending thoughts. If your pet does anything that indicates it is responding to your thoughts, the sitter needs to record the time when it occurs. Compare notes when you return home to see if your pet successfully received your thoughts.

"Do You Love Me?" Test

I have done this test successfully with both cats and dogs. You need to choose a time of day when neither you nor your pet are tired. Avoid meal times, too, as you don't want your pet to be preoccupied with thoughts of food.

Sit down somewhere comfortable and stroke and pat your pet. If your pet is small, you might have it on your lap, but it makes no difference if it's sitting or lying down beside you. Don't say anything out loud, but send loving thoughts to your pet as you stroke it. Your pet is likely to respond to both your thoughts and your actions.

Gradually, slow down and stop stroking your pet, but continue sending loving thoughts to it. Your pet may turn to look at you at this stage. Send thoughts of love for another minute or two, and then silently ask your pet a question. I usually ask: "Do you love me?" However, you might choose to ask: "Are you happy?" or "What would you like me to do for you?"

It's not necessary to close your eyes while waiting for a reply, but many people do. Remain quietly receptive to any thoughts that pop into your mind.

Your pet might respond physically. Whenever I did this test with our tabby cat, Clyde, he always answered the question "Do you love me?" by rubbing his face against my hands. He did the same thing with other members of my family when they experimented with this test.

Physical responses are easy to detect and understand. Telepathic replies can sometimes be difficult to determine. If your pet is sleepy, it might simply refuse to play the game. You might not recognize the reply, either, as it might come in the form of a feeling or a sensation, rather than words or pictures in your mind.

Naturally, you're likely to feel disappointed if you fail to get the response you expect. Dismiss these feelings right away, if they occur, as your pet is likely to sense them. Instead, simply stroke your pet and send it thoughts of love. Don't try again immediately. Wait a few hours, or maybe a day, and then try again.

It's important that you communicate with your pet as equals. Telepathic communication won't work if you talk down to an animal. J. Allen Boone visualized a two-way "mental bridge" between him and whatever animal he was communicating with. This bridge allowed thoughts to travel from him to the animal and vice versa. As long as the bridge remained horizontal, the communication was good. However, if the human end ever rose it meant he was talking down to the animal and communication ceased.[55]

This is one experiment you should repeat as frequently as possible. Your pet will look forward to it just as much as you, and you'll find it will help you both gain an even closer relationship.

Thoughts of Food Experiment

Again, this experiment should be done well away from your normal feeding times. Your pet should be in the same room as you when you first experiment with this. Once you've had practice, it makes no difference where your pet happens to be.

Sit down comfortably, close your eyes, and take ten slow, deep breaths, consciously relaxing your body each time you exhale. When you feel completely relaxed, picture or imagine that you're feeding your pet. In your mind's eye see yourself getting the food, placing it in a dish, and putting it down in the place where your pet normally eats. In your mind, visualize your pet eating the food.

Open your eyes and repeat the entire process again in your mind. "See" the entire process from reaching for the food until you see your pet eating it.

It's important that you pay no attention to your pet while doing this. You might even choose to face away from it, so you won't see your pet thinking about food.

If your pet has received your thought, it's likely to be rubbing against you or making other signs that it's time for food. Naturally, you'll have to give it a pet treat as a reward for successfully picking up your thoughts. You should probably reward yourself, too, as you and your pet have successfully engaged in interspecies telepathic communication.

---

55. J. Allen Boone, *Kinship with All Life*, 74–75 and 78–79.

Once you've succeeded with this, repeat the experiment on another day. However, this time make sure that your pet is not in the same room as you. You'll find that it will make no difference.

This experiment has a huge advantage over many others, as your pet is unlikely to ignore it unless it happens to be sound asleep or has recently eaten.

Come to Me

This is an interesting test that you can do whenever you want your pet for some reason. Instead of calling for your pet, as you would normally do, sit down comfortably, close your eyes, and think about your pet. Mentally ask it to come to you. Most of the time, your pet will arrive in a matter of minutes. If you want your pet for some purpose that it enjoys, such as going for a walk, your pet will respond immediately.

There are exceptions to this. At one time we had a Labrador dog named Bruce. He was extremely receptive to telepathic thoughts. If I so much as thought about taking him for a walk, he'd be waiting excitedly by the front door in a matter of seconds. However, if I decided it was time he had a bath, he would not respond to telepathic—or verbal—requests. Instead he'd hide, in the hope that I'd give up on the idea.

The Food Bowl Test

This is a test devised by Dr. Karlis Osis (1917–1997), an animal behaviorist and former director of research at the American Society for Psychical Research. During the 1950s, he worked at the Parapsychology Laboratory at Duke University with Dr. Rhine.

Dr. Osis conducted a series of experiments with cats in a home environment. His ten-year-old daughter, Gunta, would place an equal amount of food into two identical dishes, and then she'd will a cat to choose the dish she had chosen as a target. Over a series of trials, Gunta was able to successfully influence the actions of seven cats.[56]

Dr. Osis also performed a similar test under laboratory conditions. A kitten was placed into a T-shaped maze and an experimenter would mentally will the cat to go either left or right to follow a predetermined sequence of actions. As the results of this test proved promising, Dr. Osis took the experiment one step further. A bowl of food was placed at one end of one arm of the maze. An electric fan was used to blow away any scent of the food. This time the experimenter willed the kitten toward the food. The results obtained were well above chance level.[57]

You can replicate Gunta's test in your own home. Choose two identical dishes and place the same amount of cat food in each of them. Place one dish to the left of the doorway your cat will be using and the other the same distance to the right.

Decide which dish you want your cat to choose. Think about the dish, and repeat over and over again in your mind what you want your cat to do. If you've chosen the dish on the left, you'd silently repeat, "I want you, *(your pet's name)*, to choose the dish on your left."

Record the results. Over a period of time you'll see how successful you and your cat are at reading each other's minds.

Questions and Answers

You and your pet enjoy a close bond that encourages telepathic communication. If you haven't tried it before, you'll find it comparatively easy to enjoy silent, meaningful conversations with your pet. A good way to experiment with this is to remain receptive whenever you're playing, cuddling, or stroking your pet. Think about the love you have for your pet, and pay attention to any thoughts that pop into your

---

56. Jeane Dixon, *Do Cats Have ESP?* (New York: Aaron Publishing Group, 1998), 39–40.
57. K. Osis and E. B. Foster, "A Test of ESP in Cats," *Journal of Parapsychology* 17 (1953): 168–186.

mind. These can come in a variety of ways. You may see pictures, receive ideas, or maybe experience a feeling in your heart. You need to remain alert, as sometimes you won't realize the thought has come from your pet. Don't evaluate the thoughts until afterward. Thoughts come and go rapidly, and if you stop to analyze them you may miss much of what your pet is trying to say.

You can ask your pet specific questions during these sessions. You might silently say, "Is there anything you want to tell me?" Sometimes you'll get an immediate response. You might get a rather curt, "no." At other times you'll receive nothing at all.

When your pet answers, the reply is likely to come through pictures, body language, and sounds. Often, the reply will be just as clear as if your pet spoke to you in words. Whenever I asked our Siamese cat, Ting, what he thought of the cat next door, for instance, he'd snarl and make a high-pitched yowl. I didn't need any pictures in my mind to know exactly what he meant.

Once you've had some success with your own pet, try communicating telepathically with other people's pets. Many years ago, I used to enjoy telepathic conversations with a tabby cat I used to pass on my daily walk. I looked forward to these, and I missed him on the occasions he wasn't sitting on the fence waiting for me.

Animal communicators are people who have developed their skills at communicating telepathically with animals. Linda Thorssen, a good friend of mine, is a professional animal communicator. She asks her guardian angel to help her whenever she's working with animals. If the animal is hurt or has been abused, she visualizes it surrounded by a healing clear white light. Linda always silently asks the animal what it would like her to do to make its life better. She listens carefully and acts upon the answers. When Linda conducts workshops, she takes the participants to a zoo to expose them to as wide a range of animals as possible. She doesn't approve of zoos and circuses, but she believes she can help the animals there by listening to their stories.

Your Telepathic Dog

The tests we've already discussed can be done with a variety of animals. In this section, we'll discuss tests that are specifically for dogs.

The Color Test

This is a fascinating test that demonstrates intelligence as well as telepathy. Until comparatively recently, it was thought that dogs could see only in black and white. However, it's now known that dogs can see tints of color. They can, for instance, recognize a red ball from a blue ball. However, just like people who suffer from red-green color blindness, they find it hard to determine the colors from greenish yellow to red.[58]

You'll need six objects in different colors. I use large wooden blocks. Mine are red, blue, black, green, yellow, and white. Place these in a row and show them to your dog, picking them up one at a time and telling it what each color is. Once you've done this, show your dog one particular block several times, telling it what color it is each time. Mix the blocks, and then ask your dog to bring you the block of the color you've chosen. Once your dog can do this, repeat it with all of the other colors. Be lavish with your praise every time your dog is successful. Of course, as far as you're concerned, this is an experiment; for your dog it's a wonderful new game.

If you wish, you can take this part of the test even further. You can ask your dog to bring you the block that it likes the most. You can ask it to fetch the block that matches the clothes you're wearing.

Now it's time to turn this game into a telepathy test. Mentally choose a color and telepathically ask your dog to fetch you the block you're thinking about. Visualize your dog walking over, choosing the correct block, and bringing it back to you.

---

58. University of California at Santa Barbara, CA, "See Spot See Blue," *Scientific American* 262, no. 1 (January 1990): 87–89.

It's highly likely that your dog will seem puzzled at first. After all, up until now you've been requesting the different blocks by speaking aloud. Despite this, after a period of doubt, your dog will bring you the block you are thinking about. Praise your dog lavishly each time it's successful.

Side Visit

I was taught this fascinating test by an elderly friend who did it regularly. Every now and again, while taking her dog for its regular walk, she'd think about a place on the route where she didn't normally stop and mentally will her dog to stop there. With regular practice, she and her dog were able to do this successfully most of the time.

The first time I tried this with Bruce, I willed him to go into my sister's house. We passed it regularly, but I seldom stopped there. When we reached my sister's home, Bruce stopped, turned around to look at me, barked once, and went directly to her front door.

It was a fun test, and Bruce seemed to gain just as much pleasure from it as I did.

Where Is It?

You'll be able to conduct this experiment if your dog has a favorite, well-loved toy. When your dog is out of the room, hide the toy somewhere your dog will be able to find it. Call your dog to you and ask it to find the object.

Naturally, your dog will start by going to the place where the object is usually kept. It will probably be reluctant to look anywhere else. Think about where you've hidden the toy, and try to mentally send these thoughts to your pet. Telepathically lead it to the object step by step.

Once your dog finds the object, praise it and spend some time playing a game that involves the object.

Naturally, well-loved objects develop an odor that your dog will be able to smell. To avoid this, place the toy in an airtight container and see if your pet can still find it.

Once you start mind-to-mind communication with the animal kingdom, your life will be enhanced in many different ways. You'll have greater respect for all living things, small and large. In his book, *Kinship with All Life*, J. Allen Boone told how he communicated successfully with animals as small as flies and ants.[59] You'll become more aware of the interconnectedness between all living things, and you will realize that we are all aspects of the one Self.

In the next chapter, we'll look at the fascinating subject of telepathic dreams.

59. J. Allen Boone, *Kinship with All Life*, 145–149.

While awake, our view of ourselves is one in which we see and stress our autonomy, our individuality, our discreetness. We define our own boundaries and we try to work with them. What I'm suggesting, and which is not at all novel, is that our dreaming self is organized along a different principle. Our dreaming self is more concerned with our connection with *all* others.

—MONTAGUE ULLMAN

chapter 12

TELEPATHY IN DREAMS

More than ninety years ago, Dr. Sigmund Freud (1856–1939), the famous psychologist and creator of psychoanalysis, declared that it was an "incontestable fact that sleep creates favorable conditions for telepathy."[60] Despite this, it was another forty years before Dr. Montague Ullman (1916–2008) decided to establish the Maimonides Dream Laboratory in New York to investigate telepathy in dreams.

Even though scientific research into dream telepathy is comparatively recent, telepathic and precognitive dreams have been common throughout history. Telepathic dreams usually occur in moments of crisis. Usually, the person dreams of someone close to him or her who is in danger or who has just died.

---

60. Sigmund Freud, *Dreams and the Occult* (1922) in *New Introductory Lectures* (New York: W. W. Norton Company, 1933), 24.

An extraordinary example of this occurred in Barcelona, Spain, in 1980. One morning, an eighty-one-year-old widow named Isabel Casas visited her local police station to report a horrifying dream in which she had seen her neighbor, Rafael Perez, a fifty-six-year-old chef, "twisted in fear." In her dream, she heard a voice saying, "They are going to kill us." The police visited her home and found Rafael Perez bound and gagged in a rooftop shed on top of the block of apartments where he and Isabel Casas both lived. Perez told the police that two men had broken into his home, forced him to sign twenty-eight checks that gave his life savings to them, and said they'd return to kill him and Isabel Casas once they'd cashed the checks. The police arrested the men when they returned to the scene of the crime.[61]

Sir Henry Morton Stanley (1841–1904), the Welsh explorer who found Dr. David Livingstone, experienced a well-documented dream about the death of his Aunt Mary in 1862. When his aunt died unexpectedly in Wales, Stanley was a prisoner of the Union forces in Camp Douglas, Illinois, during the American Civil War. Several hours before she died, Stanley had a vivid dream of the tiny village in Wales where his aunt lived. In the dream, he glided to her bedside and listened to her final words of regret that she could not have helped him more. He told her that she had been as kind and good to him as she could be. He clasped her hands and heard her murmur a farewell. Stanley woke up immediately after this.[62]

The Society for Psychical Research was founded in 1882. One of the first areas they decided to investigate was telepathic dreams. They investigated 149 examples of dream telepathy and found that more than half of the dreams concerned death and a large number of others related to an emergency.

---

61. Roy Stemman, "Messages in the Mind," *The Unexplained* (London: Orbis Books, 1983), 34–37.

62. Sir Henry M. Stanley, *Autobiography of Sir Henry Morton Stanley*, ed. Dorothy Stanley (Boston: Houghton Mifflin, 1909), 207–208. There are many mentions of Stanley's dream online, including: http://www.dreamsocial.co/category/famous-dreams/.

Montague Ullman and Stanley Krippner conducted research into telepathic dreams during the 1960s and 1970s at the Maimonides Dream Laboratory in New York. In most of their tests, an experimenter would monitor the receiver, who would lie down and go to sleep. When the receiver entered the rapid eye movement (REM) stage that indicated he or she was dreaming, the experimenter used a buzzer to contact the sender, who would open an envelope and remove the image that was sealed inside. The sender would focus on this image and try to transmit it to the receiver. When the REM stage was over, the experimenter would wake the receiver, who then related the dream he or she had just experienced. This was tape-recorded and later transcribed. After this, the receiver would go back to sleep, and the process was repeated, using the same image, each time he or she entered the REM stage.

In the morning, the receiver was shown a selection of eight to twelve pictures and asked to place them in order of relevance based on his or her dream memories. In addition to this, two or three judges would listen to recordings made by the receiver each time he or she was woken, and then they tried to match them with one of the images.

The largest experiment conducted by the Maimonides Dream Laboratory took place in 1971 when two thousand people attending a Grateful Dead concert were asked to telepathically transmit a picture to Malcolm Besant, a successful English psychic, who was sleeping at the Maimonides Dream Laboratory forty-five miles away. On February 19, the randomly chosen picture showed someone sitting in the lotus position. The chakras along his spine were brightly colored and clearly visible. When Malcolm Besant woke up, he reported that he'd dreamed of talking with someone who was suspended in midair. He also said: "I'm remembering a dream I had ... about an energy box and ... a spinal column." [63]

---

63. Stanley Krippner, C. Honorton, and M. Ullman, "A long-distance ESP dream study with the Grateful Dead," *Journal of the American Society of Psychosomatic Dentistry and Medicine* 20 (1973): 9–17. See also http://stanleykrippner.weebly.com/a-pilot-study-in-dream-telepathy-with-the-grateful-dead.html. It's interesting to note that Malcolm Besant, an English psychic, is the grandson of Annie Besant, the women's rights campaigner, prolific author, and second president of the Theosophical Society.

How to Transmit a Thought
to Someone Who Is Sleeping

Ask a friend or a family member if you can attempt to send him or her a thought while he or she is asleep. Tell this person that you'll send him or her a thought at some time during the following seven nights. If the person wakes up and remembers receiving a message from you, or if you appeared in a dream, he or she should contact you.

Choose something to transmit. You might decide on a word or a phrase that means something to the other person. You might visualize a place that you both know. It doesn't matter what it is, as long as it's meaningful to both of you.

In the late evening of the day you choose to conduct the experiment, sit down quietly and spend a few minutes focusing on relaxing your entire body. Once you feel completely relaxed, think about the person you're going to send the thought to. Think about this person's good qualities and some of the happy times you've spent together. Close your eyes and visualize the person in your mind.

People visualize in different ways. You might be able to "see" the person in your mind's eye. You might not be able to see him or her, but you'll receive feelings about the person. You might "hear" this person in your mind. It doesn't matter how you experience the person, as long as you hold the visualization for as long as you can. It's time to stop when you feel the visualization is becoming faint and hard to hang on to.

Once you've done this, think of whatever it is you're trying to telepathically transmit to him or her. If it's a word or a phrase, repeat it over and over again to yourself. Imagine yourself sending this thought to your friend. If you own the object you're trying to transmit, or if you have a picture or photograph of it, open your eyes and focus on whatever it is. Again, imagine yourself telepathically transmitting the thought to your sleeping friend. Focus on this for as long as you can, and stop when you feel you've transmitted the thought successfully or when your mind starts to drift away and think about other things.

Finish by visualizing your friend again. Wish him or her a good night's sleep and express the hope that he or she will contact you in the morning.

After doing this, have something to eat and drink. I eat a few raw, unsalted almonds and drink a glass of water. Have a bath or shower, and maybe read a book for a few minutes before going to bed. You'll find it easier to fall asleep if you allow yourself a period of time between the experiment and going to bed.

Hopefully, your friend will contact you the next day. Don't tell him or her what you were transmitting until you've heard everything he or she has to say. Once you've succeeded in transmitting simple objects or thoughts, you can experiment with more complex messages.

Telepathy in Your Dreams

It is possible to tune in to other people telepathically through your dreams. Often there's a strong emotional connection that causes you to dream about a specific person and pick up his or her thoughts. Interestingly, some studies have reported that 60 to 70 percent of people who have experienced telepathy did so in their dreams.[64] In many instances, these experiences have occurred when a relative who was dying left a message with the person at the moment of death.

Telepathic dreams have been discussed for more than two thousand years. Democritus (c. 460–c. 370 BCE), the Greek philosopher, believed that dreams were "emanations" that passed from one person to another during sleep.

One of the first people in modern times to write about telepathic dreams was the Austrian psychologist and psychoanalyst Wilhelm Stekel (1868–1940). He believed that people who slept in the same room were able to influence the other person's dreams. He included several examples of telepathic dreams in his book *The Interpretation*

64. G. William Domhoff, *The Mystery of Dreams: A Search for Utopia Through Senoi Dream Therapy* (Berkeley: University of California Press, 1985), 2.

of Dreams. In one of these, a man came to see him because he was having recurring dreams in which his wife murdered their daughter. Dr. Stekel found the wife had experienced similar dreams on the same nights. They both experienced these dreams shortly before waking up in the morning.[65]

Empathic dreams are dreams in which you pick up the thoughts and emotions of someone else, usually someone who is close to you. Sometimes you'll experience the emotions as if they're happening to you. When this occurs, you'll probably wake up. More frequently, you'll be aware of the emotions happening to the other person.

A reasonably common example of an empathic dream is when someone is giving birth to a child in the middle of the night. Sometimes people close to this person will dream of her giving birth at the exact time it is occurring.

Some people experience empathic dreams regularly, while other people are unable to recall any such dreams. I can remember only one, and it involved my sister. Usually, empathic dreams are experienced by close friends and family members. However, I once met a doctor who'd had several empathic dreams about her patients.

A shared dream is when two people dream the same dream simultaneously. I've met a number of people who've told me about dreams they'd shared with partners or friends. They sometimes find it confusing, as they wonder if they are dreaming the other person's dream, or if the other person is dreaming their dream.

There are situations when it's easy to explain shared dreams. If two people have been working on the same problem during the day, they may both have similar dreams about it in their sleep. However, on other occasions there's no explanation other than telepathy.

---

65. Wilhelm Stekel, *The Interpretation of Dreams* (New York: Grosset and Dunlop, 1943), 552. Dr. Stekel also wrote a book on telepathic dreams called *Der Telepatische Traum* (Berlin: Johannes Baum Verlag, n.d.). Unfortunately, this has not been translated into English.

An interesting case concerns a young woman who dreamed that a boy had been born in a house on the opposite side of the street to her at the exact same time as the birth occurred. Because it had been a difficult birth, the stress and tension of the mother was probably picked up by the young woman in her sleep.[66]

Dr. Michael Persinger, a well-known cognitive neuroscience researcher, and Dr. Stanley Krippner, the former director of the Maimonides Dream Laboratory, analyzed the dreams of sixty-two volunteers that took place in laboratory settings. Precautions had been taken to prevent coincidence, false memories, sensory cues, and causal factors. The researchers found that the dreams that contained the greatest telepathic or clairvoyant content occurred on calm nights with low geomagnetic activity.[67]

Shared Dream Experiment

This is an interesting experiment you can do with a partner or a close friend. During the day, choose something that you would like to have appear in your dreams. This can be anything, but it's better if it's slightly unusual. You might choose a unicorn with zebra stripes or a huge, bright pink gift box that you're dying to open.

Discuss the object or topic with your partner several times during the day. You both should also think about it separately whenever you get a spare moment during the day. Picture the object in your mind while you're lying in bed waiting for sleep to come.

When you wake up in the morning, try not to move for a few minutes while you recapture any dreams you experienced. Write down or record everything you can remember.

At some stage during the day, compare notes. You may find that one or both of you cannot remember any of the dreams you had during the

---

66. C. A. Cannegieter, *Around the Dreamworld* (New York: Vantage Press, 1985), 42.

67. M. A. Persinger and S. Krippner, "Dream ESP Experiments and Geomagnetic Activity," *Journal of the American Society for Psychical Research* 83, (1989): 101–116.

night. If nothing came through about the object you'd agreed to dream about, repeat the exercise until you do.

When you both report having dreamed about the object, compare the other aspects of the dreams to see how similar your dreams were. You probably will have dreamed about the same object, but then your dreams are likely to have gone in different directions. However, if you're extremely fortunate, you may share the same dream.

Dr. Ann Faraday, a British psychologist and dream researcher, shared a dream with her husband. In her dream, she saw herself moving around their bedroom and looking out a window that had been moved to a wall that did not actually have a window. When she woke up, she told her husband about her dream. He immediately showed her the notes he'd recorded about a similar dream he'd experienced during the same night. In her husband's dream, he'd been sleeping on the wrong side of the bed, and he also noticed that the window was on the wrong wall.[68]

Lucid Dreaming

A lucid dream is a dream in which you become aware that you are dreaming. If you have ever experienced the feeling that you are actually dreaming while having a dream, you have had a lucid dream. Most people experience one or two involuntary lucid dreams during their lives. When a lucid dream occurs by chance, people usually remain passive observers of what is going on. A few people become actively involved and direct the dream wherever they wish it to go. Because it's possible to actively participate in your lucid dreams, you can use them to send thoughts to others in a very personal way.

Everyone dreams. Some people claim they don't, but this simply means they don't remember them. You are likely to have four or five dreams every night. Some may last only a minute or two, but it's pos-

---

68. Staff of Reader's Digest, *Into the Unknown* (Surry Hills, Australia: Reader's Digest Services Pty. Limited, 1982), 231.

sible for a dream to last as long as an hour. The longest and most powerful dreams occur near the end of your sleep, shortly before you wake up.

It can be a useful practice to keep a dream diary beside your bed so
you can write your dreams down before they vanish from your memory. You might prefer to record your dreams on a digital recorder. I find
it helpful to remain lying in the position I wake up in for a few minutes
and see how much of the dream I can recapture. By doing this, I am
able to recall much more of the dream than I do if I jump straight out
of bed.

A dream diary enables you to keep track of your dreams. It can be
useful to see how frequently you experience recurring dreams, and
you can make any necessary changes that may be indicated by pro-
phetic dreams. As you pay more attention to your dreams, your recall
will improve, and you'll regularly have something to record in your
dream diary. Of course, if you're woken by an alarm clock, you may
not be able to do this during the week, and you will have to experiment
on the weekends when you can wake up naturally.

Lucid dreams occur during what is known as REM sleep. REM
stands for "rapid eye movement," and is one of the five stages of sleep
we have every night. The first REM stage occurs about ninety minutes after the person falls asleep, and it lasts between five and twenty
minutes. REM periods reoccur approximately every ninety minutes
throughout the night, though the interval lessens as the night pro-
gresses and the REM stages become longer. They can last up to an hour.

One way to encourage lucid dreams is to set your alarm to go off
ninety minutes after you go to bed. When it rings, turn it off, tell yourself that you'll shortly have a lucid dream, and return to sleep.

Another method is to tell yourself several times during the day, and
again just before falling asleep, that you'll enter into a lucid dream as
soon as you see your hand, or something else that can act as a symbol,
in a dream.

Yet another method is to wait until you find yourself in the in-be-
tween stage between sleeping and waking up. As soon as you realize

you are in this state, tell yourself you'll enter into a lucid dream as soon as you see your hand (or anything else you choose to use as a symbol) in a dream. Allow yourself to drift back into a light sleep, and be ready to direct it wherever you want it to go as soon as you realize you are lucid dreaming.

Once you become aware that you're in a lucid dream, you can go anywhere and do anything. Most people travel to exotic places, have sex with a beautiful partner, or maybe do both, when they first start to lucid dream. Once that's out of the way, you might consider visiting a friend or a family member. If they're in the same time zone as you, the chances are they will be asleep. You'll see them in their bed in a state of deep repose. Once you're with them, talk normally to them, as if they were awake. Before leaving, wish them good night and tell them that they will remember you visiting them in their dreams.

Contact the person sometime during the next day and tell him or her about your lucid dream. Ask if he or she has any memory of you appearing in their dream. Sometimes you won't need to ask any questions, as they will immediately tell you that they saw you in their dreams.

Animals in Your Dreams

There is a great deal of evidence that indicates that telepathy is possible between people and animals. Sometimes this occurs in dreams. A good example of this involves the English novelist H. Rider Haggard (1856–1925). On July 7, 1904, Mrs. Haggard woke up because her husband was making sounds like a wounded animal in his sleep. She woke him, and he told her about the dream he had been having.

"I saw good old Bob [their dog] lying on his side among brushwood by water," he said. "My own personality seemed to me to be arising in some mysterious manner from the body of the dog, who lifted up his head at an unnatural angle against my face. Bob was trying to speak to me, and not being able to make himself understood by sounds, transmitted to my mind in an undefined fashion the knowledge that he was dying."[69]

Bob's collar was found, bloodstained, the following morning on a railway bridge. Four days after the dream, Bob was found dead, floating in a river. He had been struck by a train on the bridge and had fallen into the water.

Hopefully, any dreams you have about your pet will be pleasant ones.

Going to Sleep Telepathy

In my early twenties, I worked as a sales representative for a large publishing company in the United Kingdom. This gave me the opportunity to explore large parts of a country that was new to me while traveling to visit my customers. I'd frequently be away from home for a week at a time, and I enjoyed the evenings in the hotels chatting with other sales representatives over a pint or two of beer.

I became friends with another sales rep who was about my age. Once Peter discovered my interest in the psychic world, he told me that he communicated telepathically with his grandmother, who lived in Spain. Each night, when he went to bed, he'd close his eyes and send a telepathic message to her. Sometimes he'd receive no reply, and this meant that she was already asleep. However, most nights she'd be lying in her bed waiting to hear from him. She'd immediately reply to Peter's message, and then they'd enjoy a telepathic conversation for about twenty minutes.

Peter told me that they'd started doing this a few years earlier after he'd been to visit her. She'd complained that she'd found it hard to get to sleep since her husband had died, and she missed the bedtime chat

---

69. H. Rider Haggard, quoted in the *Journal of the Society for Psychical Research* (October 1904). This story can also be found in Nandor Fodor, *Encyclopaedia of Psychic Science* (London: Arthurs Press, 1933). Reprinted by New Hyde Park: University Books, Inc., 1966, 377.

they had before they both fell asleep. Half jokingly, Peter said that he'd send her a message when he went to bed that night.

Unfortunately, Peter forgot to do this. A few nights later, after he'd returned to London, he was lying in bed when he received a message from his grandmother.

"It couldn't have been anyone else," he told me. "It was a message in my mind, but it was in her voice. I could almost hear her saying the words."

Peter felt a little bit stupid, but he sent her a message in reply. To his amazement, his grandmother made a comment about it, and then she asked him how his flight had been.

"That was the start of it," he told me. "Almost every night since then, we have a nice little chat, and she falls asleep. I can tell when it's going to happen, so I have time to say good night before she's fully asleep."

Peter hadn't told anyone about these communications, as he thought they'd think he was crazy. "Sometimes I think I am," he told me. "I've never heard of anyone else doing this. Have you?" At the time I hadn't, but I've met many people since who have the ability to communicate telepathically with loved ones when they're away from home.

I told Peter that I'd try it out for myself. "You'd better not get yourself a girlfriend then," he said. "What would she think if she was tucked up in bed with you and you started chatting telepathically with someone else?"

I began experimenting right away. I wasn't able to communicate with family while lying in bed at night, as they were all on the other side of the world. I found I could sometimes make contact with friends I'd made in the United Kingdom, and I was able to confirm that when they contacted me the next day to say they'd been about to drop off to sleep and they'd suddenly thought of me. However, it wasn't until several months after I'd returned to New Zealand that I started experimenting with it again.

I'd met a middle-aged woman from Russia who was extremely interested in extrasensory perception. Because of our shared interests, we became good friends, and I suggested we try communicating telepathically while lying in bed waiting to fall asleep.

On the first night, we started well, and exchanged greetings and a few comments. After that, apart from an awareness of each other, nothing else came through. We tried a week later, with only partial success. My friend suggested that we wait a while before doing any more as she was having problems in her relationship. A few nights after that, I woke an hour or so after falling asleep with a feeling of deep sadness. I felt so heavy I could hardly move.

As everything was going well in my life, I immediately thought of my friend and the problems she was having. I sent her messages of friendship and my willingness to help in any way I could. After several minutes, the feeling disappeared, and I was able to fall asleep again feeling certain that my friend was all right.

She phoned me the next morning to thank me for my help. Her message to me had been so strong that it woke me up, and I was grateful that my reply had reached her and proved helpful.

She and her husband managed to resolve their problems, and I lost contact with them when they moved to Australia some months later.

If you would like to experiment with this, find someone who lives in the same time zone as you and who goes to bed at roughly the same time that you do. Start by thinking about the person you're going to communicate with, and see if you can make contact telepathically. You'll probably become aware of each other immediately, but it might take a few nights before you can exchange any messages. Don't try to rush the process. Be patient, and allow it to take as long as necessary for you and your friend to communicate successfully before falling asleep.

In the next chapter, we'll look at how psychic readers can utilize mind reading to enhance their readings. You'll find this interesting and useful, even if you have no intention of ever giving a reading.

Your thoughts are transparent.

—WAYNE GERALD TROTMAN

chapter 13

TELEPATHY AND THE PSYCHIC READER

When psychic readers give someone a reading, they regularly pick up flashes of intuition for their clients. Usually, these appear spontaneously, possibly when the client is thinking about a particular concern. If the reader is feeling energetic and isn't tired, the thought will appear in his or her mind and can be used to help provide a useful and insightful reading. However, if it's near the end of the day and the psychic reader has been busy, he or she is likely to feel exhausted. In this state, he or she would probably fail to pick up all of the subliminal telepathic messages that the clients are sending to him or her.

Many years ago, when I read palms in shopping malls, I'd read up to one hundred palms a day. These were quick readings that were about five minutes long. I wanted to give good readings to everyone, but by the end of the day I felt drained of energy, and it was difficult to receive psychic messages that I could give to all of the later clients. Fortunately, it's possible to read palms scientifically, and I was able to provide satisfactory readings by simply reading the shape, lines, and other markings on the palm of each client's hand. Although it's possible to do good palm readings this way, you can provide much better readings when you also access your intuition. Consequently, the people who had readings from me in the mornings were likely to have received better readings than the people who came later in the day. It took me a long time to find a simple answer to this problem.

When someone sat down at my table for a reading, I'd hold both of their hands and ask them to stare into my eyes and think about the main reason why they wanted a reading. Within thirty seconds, I'd telepathically receive the necessary information and be able to start the reading. By doing this, my final clients of the day received readings that were just as good as those who had seen me in the morning. The other benefit of doing this was that everyone enjoyed the process, and it helped me gain instant rapport with every client.

I quickly learned to tell my clients any hunches, feelings, or insights I gained, no matter how strange they seemed to be. Sometimes they seemed so outlandish that I'd start by saying, "I've just had a feeling, and it makes no sense to me, but I feel I should say it." Naturally, not all the feelings I received made much sense to my clients, but a large percentage did. Occasionally, clients called me later to tell me that something I'd told them that made no sense at the time had happened or that they now understood what it was all about.

If you give readings for others, for fun or as a business, you'll find they'll become much more insightful and helpful if you make use of your inborn ability to read minds.

Eye to Eye

It's impossible for two people to gaze into each other's eyes for any length of time without becoming totally attuned to each other. I like to hold hands with the other person while I do this, but this is not essential. Simply quiet your mind, gaze gently into the person's eyes, and remain receptive to any thoughts or insights that come to you.

Rumi (1207–1273), the Persian poet, knew the power of gazing into a lover's eyes, and many of his poems mention this. As eyes are considered "windows to the soul," it's not surprising that a great deal of powerful information can come from gazing deeply into someone's eyes.

Ask the Source

Many readers feel they need to adhere to the philosophy of "see all, know all." Consequently, they prefer to give their readings with as little input from their clients as possible. This is a mistake, as no one can possibly know everything.

There's nothing wrong with asking the client what his or her problem is. Let's assume Kathy, your client, asks, "Will my relationship with Jason continue to develop?"

"Let me ask the Source," you reply. Hold out both hands palms upward, close your eyes, and wait for a response.

Frequently, you'll pick up the client's thoughts—Kathy's in this case. While you're waiting for a reply from the Source, Kathy will be thinking about her relationship, and you're likely to pick up some of her hopes and dreams, as well as her doubts and concerns. You're likely to also receive insight from the Source.

When you've obtained the information you need, open your eyes, and tell Kathy what insights you picked up.

Write Down Your Concerns

The reader hands the client a pen and paper and asks him or her to write down everything he or she would like to have covered in the course of the reading. The reader can leave the room while the client does this. When the reader returns, he or she asks the client to slowly and silently read through the list three times. The client then folds the sheet of paper and puts it away.

As the client reads through his or her list of problems and concerns, the reader sits quietly and remains receptive to any information and insights that appear in his or her mind.

The Journey Reading

In the Journey Reading, the reader takes the client on an imaginary journey that provides insights into a particular problem or concern that the client has. Most of the time, the client will receive answers from the experience. At the same time, the reader will also receive insights about the client's difficulties, and these can be discussed after the journey has taken place.

Ask the client to sit in a comfortable recliner-type chair and close his or her eyes. I usually cover the client with a blanket. This helps keep the client warm, but more importantly, it provides him or her with a sense of security during the process.

Once the client has his or her eyes closed, you take him or her through a relaxation process. Then, guide the client on an imaginary journey to visit a wise man/woman/oracle who can provide insights into the client's concerns. Once the client has finished talking to the oracle, he or she returns to the present, and you can discuss what happened during the journey and the insights he or she gained from the experience.

Whenever possible, I like to guide my clients to a place they would like to visit. I've taken people to Tibet, Venus, Lourdes, a South Sea island, Mu, Atlantis, and a variety of other places. If the client doesn't have a preference, I'll take him or her to whatever place seems right to me at the time.

Each reading is different, and I frequently surprise myself with what I come out with during the journey. As many of my clients express a desire to visit Atlantis, we'll go there on this sample journey.

Take a nice deep breath in, and allow your eyes to close as you exhale.
Let all your muscles relax. Each breath takes you deeper and deeper

into a nice, calm, peaceful relaxed state. In a few moments you'll take three deep breaths, and each time you exhale you'll go deeper and deeper and deeper. Take the first deep breath. Relaxation in, and tension and stress out. That's good. Nice, even deep breaths. Take another deep breath now, and feel all the stress and tension fade away as you exhale. That's good. And now the third deep breath. That's good. Hold it for the count of three. One … two … three … and exhale. Feel the gentle relaxation spreading throughout your body. Nothing need bother or disturb you as you listen to the sound of my voice. Each breath takes you deeper and deeper, and you'll soon become totally and completely relaxed.

Forget about your breathing now and simply become aware of just how loose, limp, and relaxed you are. Feel all the tension and stress leave your body each time you exhale. It's so pleasant to relax deeply like this, with nothing to concern or bother you. All you need do is simply listen to the sound of my voice and allow yourself to relax more and more and more.

And you can keep on going deeper now, feeling exactly like a rag doll that's had all the tension and strain wrung out of it. You're becoming loose and limp, and so, so relaxed. Allow this pleasant relaxation to drift all through your body, starting in your feet and gradually drifting up into your legs and thighs. It's moving into your abdomen and chest now, and as you relax even more it drifts into your arms, your shoulders, and your neck. It's drifting into your face now, and you feel more relaxed and at peace than you've ever felt before. Allow the muscles around your eyes to relax. They're the finest muscles in your whole body, and as they relax, you'll feel every part of your body relaxing even more than before.

That's good, that's very, very good. And now, in this nice, calm, peaceful relaxed state, I'd like you to focus solely on my voice as we get ready to pay a visit to the mystical continent of Atlantis. I've guided many people there, and they've all gained insights and knowledge from the experience.

To start with, I'd like you to imagine that you're out in the country somewhere. It might be a place you've visited in the past, or it could be an imaginary place that you create in your mind. It makes no difference. Picture yourself, sitting or lying down, in this calm and peaceful scene. It's a beautiful, sunny summer's day, and you can feel the gentle warmth of the sun and sense a very slight gentle breeze. You look upward at the clear blue sky and notice a few fluffy clouds gliding slowly across the sky. You can hear the song of birds in a nearby grove of trees, and one or two particularly beautiful birds fly overhead. You find it hard to comprehend the sheer tranquility and beauty of the scene you're in. It's so peaceful, and so, so relaxing.

As you're lying there, you sense that someone is walking out of the grove of trees. You turn to look, and you see a tall man dressed in white robes and carrying a long staff heading toward you. You feel perfectly calm and relaxed, as you can sense an aura of goodness and gentleness emanating from him. As he gets closer, you can see he has a beautiful smile that suffuses his entire face. His eyes are kind, yet penetrating. He is even taller than you thought, and as he stops in front of you, you realize that he must be at least seven feet tall.

You stand up and shake his hand. "My name's Ethor," he says. "I understand you wish to visit Atlantis. I'm happy to guide you there and bring you back again after you've gained the answers you seek." "Thank you," you reply. "How do we get there?" Ethor points up into the sky. You look up and see a silver, cylindrical spaceship hovering overhead. You gasp in amazement as it slowly descends and lands gently on the grass in front of you. After a few moments, a door on the side of the spaceship opens. It turns into a ramp that smoothly lowers itself down to the ground. Ethor gestures toward the spacecraft, and you both walk on board. It seems natural to do this, and you feel totally relaxed as you walk up the ramp and into the spacecraft. You both sit down in comfortable armchairs and watch the ramp close. After a few seconds, the spaceship silently rises into the sky.

"Who's controlling this spaceship?" you ask.

Ethor laughs. "It doesn't need a pilot, the way you do here on Earth. One of my friends in Atlantis is guiding it with the power of his mind."

"How long will the journey take?" you ask.

"We're almost there," Ethor says. "Travel is almost instantaneous on this ship."

He was right. In just seconds the spaceship has flown from your beautiful country landscape to the sunken world of Atlantis. The spaceship is so quiet that you don't even hear it land in Atlantis. After a few seconds, the door opens again, and Ethor leads the way out of the spacecraft.

Atlantis wasn't quite what you expected. You find yourself standing on a hill overlooking a futuristic-looking city. The inhabitants seemed to be traveling everywhere in oval pods that fly rapidly from place to place. A few rocks and seashells on the ground are the only indications that you're underwater—at least you think you must be.

"Take as long as you like to become familiar with Atlantis," Ethor says. "When you're ready, I'll take you to see our High Priest. He already knows the answers to all your questions." You look around, fascinated with everything you see. You feel a sense of anticipation, knowing that you're about to meet the High Priest. You sigh deeply and tell Ethor that you're ready.

"Take a deep breath and close your eyes," Ethor says. "One, two, three. Now open them again." You open your eyes and see that you've been somehow transported into a large, mysterious-looking cave. You can hear water in the distance. Despite being underground, the cave is as light as day, but you can't see any form of artificial lighting. "This way," Ethor says. You follow him as he walks deeper into the cave. The lighting gradually changes and everything is suffused with a beautiful golden glow. You suddenly see a magnificent throne, and it seems a little strange to see it sitting there in the middle of a cave. In front of it are several cushions. "Sit down," Ethor says. "I'll be back when you're ready." You start to thank him, but he's vanished. You turn

back to the throne, and you see that an imposing-looking man is now sitting on it. Like Ethor, he's extremely tall and wears white robes, but he also has a gold sash that runs diagonally across his chest. His hair is silvery white, his smile is welcoming, and his blue eyes twinkle with pleasure at seeing you.

You probably look surprised, as the man says, "Hello, my child. Welcome to Atlantis." His voice is quiet, gentle, and incredibly deep. Like Ethor, he has a beautiful, serene smile. His entire body is surrounded by a rich gold aura. He waits until you've sat down and are feeling more at home in this strange environment. "I'm pleased that you've come to me for advice," he says. "I've been following your progress for a long time. Please, tell me what's on your mind."

You start to speak, telling him about your problems and concerns. You feel totally at ease, and you talk with the High Priest as if you were old friends. You sense that you could tell him anything, and he'd give you good, helpful insights in response. Please, in your mind, ask him anything you wish. He wants to help you.

At this point, you stop talking for at least sixty seconds. Relax and remain receptive to any thoughts or insights that come into your mind. Most of these thoughts will come from your client. When you feel your client has received all the information he or she needs, you can start talking again.

Have you received the answers you seek? (Pause until your client makes some acknowledgment. Give him or her more time, if necessary.) *You thank the High Priest for all his help and advice. He smiles gently and says, "Come and see me again whenever you need help or advice. You're welcome to come and see me anytime you wish." You hear a sound and find that Ethor has returned to take you back home. You turn back to the throne to thank the High Priest again, but he's vanished as quickly as he arrived.*

You feel very grateful for all the help you've received, and you struggle to tell Ethor how valuable it has all been. "It's our pleasure," Ethor says. *"I wish more people would ask us for help. You all seem to need it. Please take a deep breath and close your eyes. One, two, three. And now, open them again when you're ready."* *You open your eyes and find you're back in the spacecraft. Seconds later, the door opens and Ethor gives you a hug.* *"Please come and visit us whenever you wish,"* *he says.*

You thank him before walking down the ramp and back into your beautiful country scene. The door silently closes behind you, and you turn just in time to see the spacecraft disappearing into the sky. You find a comfortable spot on the grass to lie down on.

In this comfortable place you can reflect on everything you've learned. You remember absolutely everything that happened during your journey. You've enjoyed it, but it's also good to be back home again.

In a moment, I'm going to count from one to five. As soon as I start counting, you'll be back in my office feeling relaxed and peaceful. When I reach five, you'll open your eyes and feel absolutely wonderful.

One, feeling better than you've felt in years. Two, gaining energy and feeling fine. Three, feeling happy and contented. Four, becoming a little bit excited now. And five, eyes opening and feeling great.

I generally remain silent for about sixty seconds to give the client time to get used to being back in the real world again. He or she is usually thrilled with the experience. Some become emotional, as it's a powerful experience, especially if the client has gained useful insights into what is going on in his or her life.

We discuss the experience, and I ask if the client has learned everything he or she needs to know. Usually, the client is happy to tell me what he or she learned, and I add any thoughts or insights that occurred to me during the journey. Sometimes the client doesn't want to discuss what happened on the trip, and that's fine, too.

I may, or may not, give the client a palm or tarot reading after the journey. It's not necessary if the client has gained all the information he or she requires. However, it can sometimes be helpful to use the reading to expand on what came through on the journey and to provide insights into other areas of the client's life.

Although the Journey Reading requires only that the client be relaxed, afterward many people feel that they've been hypnotized. This may well be the case, as hypnosis is simply an altered state of consciousness. Every time you have a daydream, you're in a state of hypnosis. You may sometimes go on "autopilot" when driving home from work, and then you wonder how you got there. This means you were in a state of what's called "wild hypnosis." You were driving safely, and would have been able to react instantly if anything cropped up while you were in this state. If you cry during a sad movie, you're also in a state of hypnosis. You know that the movie is only a picture projected onto the screen, but because you've become emotionally involved, you're actually hypnotized.

The sole purpose of giving a reading to someone is to help the person as much as possible. Consequently, you need to encourage mind-to-mind communication in this situation to enable you to provide the best reading you can.

I should mention that offering Journey Readings to your clients is an excellent way to build up your reading practice. It's something novel and different that you can offer, and it will set you apart from all the other readers in your area. You'll find many clients will return solely to have a Journey Reading. They'll also talk about their journeys to friends and colleagues at work. Some of these people will also want readings from you, and your business will continue to grow and expand.

Don't try to comprehend with your mind.
Your minds are very limited. Use your intuition.
—MADELEINE L'ENGLE

chapter 14

MIND READING
IN EVERYDAY LIFE

You'll find many opportunities to practice your mind-reading skills in everyday life. You may find you're already doing this without realizing it. Every time you meet someone you subconsciously assess him or her using your innate body language skills. In a fraction of a second, you pick up and act on the other person's facial expressions, movements, tone of voice, mood, and intentions. When you become good at this, you'll demonstrate what is known as "empathic accuracy." This is a term coined by Dr. William Ickes, Distinguished Professor of Psychology at the University of Texas at Arlington, in 1988. It describes someone who is extremely good at intuiting other people's feelings, moods, thoughts, and motivations. Some people do this naturally, but it's a skill that anyone can develop. If you work in teaching, healing, human resources, or sales, you're likely to have developed empathic accuracy and use this ability on a daily basis.

Another way to use your mind-reading ability in everyday life occurs if you want someone to contact you. If you're unable to contact the person by phone or e-mail, you might send your desire out into the universe and probably not even realize that you're doing it.

Thinking of someone and then bumping into him or her shortly afterward is another example of sending your thoughts out and having them received by someone else. Not long ago, I thought of someone I hadn't seen in years, and I received a Facebook message from him just a few hours later.

On several occasions, I've received intuitions that enabled me to avoid potentially difficult situations. I've learned the hard way to always follow my intuition—or my gut instincts, as some people call it. I have no idea if I received these warnings about potential danger by picking up someone's thoughts, or if I became aware of them by some other means. No matter how I receive them, I always act on my hunches and feelings.

One of the most useful ways to practice mind reading is to send thoughts of friendship and love to the people you care about. These people may not always let you know that they felt your blessing on them, but you'll notice your relationships with each of them will become smoother and closer than ever before.

How to Send Love to Someone

With practice, you'll be able to send love whenever you wish. However, like everything else in this book, it takes practice to become good at it. Consequently, when you start experimenting with this you should set aside about twenty minutes for this exercise.

All you need is a comfortable chair or bed. I prefer to do this exercise in a recliner. I find I fall asleep far too easily if I try to do this in bed. Make yourself as comfortable as you can. Close your eyes and take a few slow, deep breaths to help you relax. I usually start by taking myself through a relaxation exercise, but this isn't strictly necessary as the entire process is relaxing.

When you feel comfortable, think about the person you're going to send love to. You might picture him or her doing something enjoyable or possibly recall the last time the two of you were together. Everyone is different. You might be able to clearly see this person in your mind's eye. You might not be able to "see" him or her, but you may sense that person's energy or maybe hear his or her voice. You might simply think about the person. It makes no difference how you experience the person you're going to send love to, just as long as you're able to focus on the image or thought of him or her.

Once the person is in your mind, tell yourself that you're going to telepathically send unconditional love to him or her. To do this, start by thinking of the love you have for this person. Allow this love to build up in the area of your heart. When you feel your heart is full of love, take a deep breath and, as you exhale, visualize the love gently flowing from your heart and traveling instantly to your special person. It doesn't matter where in the world he or she may be. He or she might be sitting quietly beside you, totally unaware of the exercise you're doing. He or she may be thousands of miles away. It makes no difference if the person is asleep or awake. If you're familiar with the chakras, you might prefer to send the love from your heart chakra rather than from your heart. As it makes no difference to the recipient, you should use whatever method feels better for you.

Picture this person receiving your love and gaining energy and pleasure from it. Continue sending love until you sense that the person has received enough. This will vary from person to person. You'll notice that even the same person will accept different amounts of love from time to time. This is perfectly natural, and there's no need to try to force more love to someone who has received enough.

You may also find that on some occasions you seem to have limitless love in your heart that you can send. At other times, you might have to stop for a minute or two to allow more love to come into your heart.

Once the person has received enough love, stop sending it and start thinking about your love for the person instead. When you feel ready, smile and mentally say goodbye to the person. Open your eyes and carry on with your day. If you're doing this in bed at night, sigh deeply and allow yourself to drift off into sleep.

In this exercise, you're sending your love to someone else. You may feel that this is purely a one-sided process. However, this isn't the case. As a result of doing this exercise on a regular basis, you'll notice that your relationship with the other person will become closer, warmer, and better than ever before. There'll be more harmony, and you'll feel fulfilled and happy.

You cannot do this exercise too often. It can be extremely beneficial if you're experiencing problems in your relationship or if your partner is unwell. It is also useful if your relationship is suffering from a lack of communication or trust.

Obviously, you should do this exercise for the special people in your life. However, you can also send love and friendship to people you'd like to become closer to or want to know better.

It can also be useful to send love to people you have problems and difficulties with. You'll find that sending thoughts of love to them will enhance the relationship, and you'll find you'll be able to get on with them much more easily and harmoniously than ever before.

You can also send telepathic messages of love instantly whenever you wish. You already do this whenever you think fondly of someone. To do this consciously, all you need do is think how much you love someone and gently send the thought to that person. This has the advantage that you can send your message anywhere you happen to be. You might be able to send several messages of love while waiting in line or while waiting for a traffic light to change.

Sending Love and Friendship to Strangers

You can use the previous experiment to send love to anyone. They don't need to be close friends or family members. If you hear that someone is ill, for instance, you could send love and healing thoughts to him or her. You can send love to an acquaintance who is looking for work or experiencing problems of some sort. You can even send love to people you don't like. You'll find this will rapidly improve the relationship.

You can send thoughts of any sort. Not long ago, I sent thoughts of encouragement to a young man who is trying to make a career in his sport, but he was finding it hard to get started. Shortly afterward, he was picked up by a small club and is about to start living his dream.

Most people are surprised when I suggest that they send positive thoughts to complete strangers. This is not as weird as it may sound. Recently, I spoke with a rather serious man who habitually has a grumpy expression on his face. He told me that he felt happy inside, but his face failed to recognize the fact. A few years ago, he walked into a store to buy something and noticed a look of fear on the shop assistant's face. There and then, he resolved to change his expression. Now, whenever he enters a store, or business premises of any sort, he smiles before walking in. He says that doing this has changed his life, because the smile makes him appear friendly and people enjoy dealing with him.

This man changed the attitude that strangers had toward him by changing his facial expression. You can do the same, and much more, by smiling while sending a telepathic message of friendship to the person you're about to deal with.

Imagine you've had a difficult day. On your way home, you decide to go into a store to buy something you need. As the day hasn't brought you any joy, you're unlikely to make the effort to engage in casual conversation, and you may barely notice the cashier as you hand over the item for scanning. Because of this, the cashier may handle the transaction in virtual silence, and you'll leave taking your bad mood with you.

Let's imagine a different scenario. It's at the end of the same difficult day, and you're in the store to buy the item. Before you get to the checkout, you look at the cashier and think for a moment about the day she's probably had. She will have served many people, and she is likely to feel tired. She might have felt stressed at times, and she may have had to serve a number of rude, inconsiderate people.

Before approaching her, you send her thoughts of friendship and gratitude for the work she does. Do you think this will make any difference? Even if she doesn't pick up your thought, the act of sending it certainly will help you, as you've now empathized with the cashier and seen her as a living person with hopes, dreams, and ambitions. You'll probably smile and make a comment or two as she processes the transaction. All of this will make the cashier feel appreciated, and she'll probably give you a smile in return.

However, all of that is a bonus for you, as she'll have subliminally picked up your silent telepathic message and will feel better about herself and the work she's doing.

You can do this to everyone you encounter in your everyday life. Try it with as many people as you can for a week or two and see what difference it makes to you and the people who receive your good thoughts.

One person truly can make a difference.

One mind can act at a distance upon another, without the habitual
medium of words, or any other visible means of communication.
—CAMILLE FLAMMARION

CONCLUSION

I hope you've enjoyed learning about mind reading, and you and your partner are working your way through the different experiments. You'll find your new skills will prove useful in every aspect of your life. In fact, you may already have demonstrated some of these skills to others. I hope you'll encourage like-minded people to look at mind reading, too. However, choose these people with care, as not everyone will understand your interest, and you're bound to encounter people who have totally closed minds on the subject.

This has always been the case. Dr. Sigmund Freud believed in telepathy, and called it "thought transference." However, despite his belief in mind reading, he was cautious, and he came to the conclusion that thought transference needed to be kept as a psychoanalytic secret. This was because he felt it would be disastrous for the new science of psychoanalysis if thought transference, or mind reading, became public knowledge.

In a letter Freud wrote to Sándor Ferenczi (1873–1933), a Hungarian psychoanalyst, he said: "Keep quiet about it [thought transference] for the time being, we will have to engage in future experiments." [70] Despite urging secrecy on others, Freud was so fascinated with the subject that he ultimately wrote six papers on thought transference. Toward the end of his life, Freud came to the conclusion that if he had his life to live over again, he would possibly devote it to the study of thought transference. In a letter to Hereward Carrington (1880–1958), an eminent author and psychic researcher, Freud wrote: "I am not one of those who from the outset disapprove of the study of the so-called occult psychological phenomena as unscientific, as unworthy or even as dangerous. If I were at the beginning of a scientific career, instead of as now at its end, I would perhaps choose no other field of work in spite of all difficulties." [71]

It's important to be cautious and not accept everything at face value. Experiment, test, and ask questions. Only then make up your own mind. Even Eileen Garrett, the influential Irish medium and parapsychologist, had doubts at times. When she was asked if she believed in all the psychic subjects she'd studied, she said: "Monday, Wednesday, and Friday, I do. Tuesday, Thursday, and Saturday, I don't. On Sunday, I don't give a damn." [72]

I wish you great success as you continue with your studies in mind reading.

---

70. Eva Brabant, Ernst Falzeder, and Patrizia Giampier-Deutsch, *The Correspondence of Sigmund Freud and Sándor Ferenczi* (Cambridge, MA: Harvard University Press, 1993), 79.

71. Sigmund Freud, "Unpublished Letter on Psychology to Hereward Carrington," *Psychoanalysis and the Future: A Centenary Commemoration of the Birth of Sigmund Freud* (New York: National Psychological Association for Psychoanalysis, Inc., 1957), 12.

72. Sioban Roberts, "Legendary Psychic's Journal Gets Reincarnated," *The National Post* (Toronto), April 7, 2001.

SUGGESTED READING

Atkinson, William Walker. *Practical Mind-Reading: A Course of Lessons on Thought-Transference, Telepathy, Mental-Currents, Mental Rapport, etc.* Chicago: Advanced Thought Publishing, 1908.

Auerbach, Loyd. *Psychic Dreaming: A Parapsychologist's Handbook.* New York: Warner Books, 1991.

Boone, J. Allen. *Kinship with All Life.* New York: Harper & Row, 1954.

Burnham, Sophy. *The Art of Intuition: Cultivating Your Inner Wisdom.* New York: Jeremy P. Tarcher/Penguin, 2011.

Butler, W. E. *An Introduction to Telepathy.* New York: Weiser, 1975.

Caudill, Maureen. *Impossible Realities: The Science Behind Energy Healing, Telepathy, Reincarnation, Precognition, and Other Black Swan Phenomena.* Charlottesville, VA: Hampton Roads Publishing, 2012.

Clegg, Brian. *Extra Sensory: The Science and Pseudoscience of Telepathy and Other Powers of the Mind.* New York: St. Martin's Press, 2013.

Cooper, Joe. *The Mystery of Telepathy.* London: Constable and Company Limited, 1982.

Darwin, Charles. *The Expression of the Emotions in Man and Animals.* London: John Murray and Company, 1872.

Edmunds, Simeon. *Hypnotism and Psychic Phenomena.* North Hollywood, CA: Wilshire Book Company, 1961.

Epley, Nicholas. *Mindwise: How We Understand What Others Think, Believe, Feel and Want.* New York: Alfred A. Knopf, 2014.

Finnegan, Ruth. *Communicating: The Multiple Modes of Human Communication*. Abingdon, UK, and New York: Routledge, Second ed. 2014.

Gackenbach, Jayne, and Jane Bosveld. *Control Your Dreams: How Lucid Dreaming Can Help You Uncover Your Hidden Desires, Confront Your Hidden Fears, and Explore the Frontiers of Human Consciousness*. New York: HarperCollins, 1989.

Goldberg, Lewis R., and Tina K. Rosolack. "The Big Five Factor Structure as an Integrative Framework: An Empirical Comparison with Eysenck's P-E-N Model." In *The Developing Structure of Temperament and Personality from Infancy to Adulthood*, edited by C. F. Halverson Jr., G. A. Kohnstamn, and R. P. Martin, 7–35. New York: Erlbaum, 1994. http://projects.ori.org/lrg/PDFs_papers/BigFive-PEN.pdf.

Ickes, William. *Everyday Mind Reading: Understanding What Other People Think and Feel*. Buffalo, NY: Prometheus Books, 2003.

Inglis, Brian, with Ruth West and the Koestler Foundation. *The Unknown Guest: The Mystery of Intuition*. London: Chatto & Windus, 1987.

Kaplan, Michael, and Ellen Kaplan. *Chances Are …: Adventures in Probability*. New York: Penguin Books, 2006.

Krippner, Stanley, editor. *Dreamtime & Dreamwork: Decoding the Language of the Night*. Los Angeles: Jeremy P. Tarcher, 1990.

LeShan, Lawrence. *The Medium, the Mystic, and the Physicist*. New York: Viking Press, 1974.

McGill, Ormond. *Real Mental Magic*. Calgary, Canada: Hades Publications, 1989.

Nikolic, Seka, with Sarah Tay. *You Know More Than You Think: How to Access Your Super-Subconscious Powers*. London: Hay House UK, 2010.

Ostrander, Sheila, and Lynn Schroeder. *PSI: Psychic Discoveries Behind the Iron Curtain*. London: Sphere Books Limited, 1973.

Playfair, Guy Lyon. *If This Be Magic: The Forgotten Power of Hypnosis.* London: Jonathan Cape Limited, 1985.

_____ . *Twin Telepathy: The Psychic Connection.* London: Vega Books, 2002.

Powell, Diane Hennacy. *The ESP Enigma: The Scientific Case for Psychic Phenomena.* New York: Walker & Company, 2009.

Pratt, J. G., J. B. Rhine, Burke M. Smith, Charles E. Stuart, and Joseph A. Greenwood. *Extra-Sensory Perception After Sixty Years.* New York: Henry Holt and Company, 1940.

Radin, Dean. *Supernormal: Science, Yoga, and the Evidence for Extraordinary Psychic Abilities.* New York: Deepak Chopra Books, 2013.

Rao, K. Ramakrishna. *Experimental Parapsychology: A Review and Interpretation.* Springfield, IL: Charles C. Thomas, 1966.

Rhine, J. B. *Extra-Sensory Perception.* Boston: Boston Society for Psychic Research, 1934.

_____ . *New Frontiers of the Mind: The Story of the Duke Experiments.* New York: Farrar & Rinehart, 1937.

Schwarz, Berthold. *Parent-Child Telepathy: A Study of the Telepathy of Everyday Life.* New York: Garrett Publications, 1972.

Sheldrake, Rupert. *Dogs That Know When Their Owners Are Coming Home and Other Unexplained Powers of Animals.* London: Hutchinson and Company, 1999.

_____ . *Seven Experiments That Could Change the World: A Do-It-Yourself Guide to Revolutionary Science.* New York: Riverhead, 1995.

Sinclair, Upton. *Mental Radio: Does It Work and How?* Monrovia, CA: Self-published, 1930.

Slate, Joe H. *Psychic Empowerment: A 7-Day Plan for Self-Development.* St. Paul, MN: Llewellyn Publications, 1995.

Smedley, Jenny. *Pets Have Souls Too.* Carlsbad, CA: Hay House, 2009.

Smith, Penelope. *Animal Talk: Interspecies Telepathic Communication*. Hillsboro, OR: Beyond Words Publishing, 1999.

Soal, S. G., and F. Bateman. *Modern Experiments in Telepathy*. London: Faber & Faber, 1954.

Soal, S. G., and H. T. Bowden. *The Mind Readers*. London: Faber & Faber, 1959.

Spiegel, Murray R., Seymour Lipschutz, and John Liu. *Mathematical Handbook of Formulas and Tables*. Schaum's Outline Series. New York: McGraw-Hill, 2013.

Targ, Russell, and Harold Puthoff. *Mind-Reach*. London: Jonathan Cape Limited, 1977.

Tart, Charles T. *Learning to Use Extrasensory Perception*. Chicago: University of Chicago Press, 1976.

Ullman, Montague, Stanley Krippner, and Alan Vaughan. *Dream Telepathy: Experiments in Nocturnal ESP*. New York: Macmillan, 1973.

Vasiliev, Leonid L. *Experiments in Distant Influence*. London, Wildwood House, 1976.

———. *Mysterious Phenomena of the Human Psyche*. New Hyde Park: University Books, 1965.

Volk, Steve. *Fringe-ology: How I Tried to Explain Away the Unexplainable*. New York: HarperCollins, 2011.

Warcollier, René. *Experiments in Telepathy*. Translated by Josephine B. Gridley. Boston: Boston Society for Psychic Research, 1938.

———. *Mind to Mind*. Translated by Josephine B. Gridley, E. de P. Matthews, and Herma Briffault. New York: Collier Books, 1963.

Webster, Richard. *Body Language Quick & Easy*. Woodbury, MN: Llewellyn Publications, 2014.

———. *Face Reading Quick & Easy*. Woodbury, MN: Llewellyn Publications, 2012.

_____ . *Is Your Pet Psychic? Developing Psychic Communication with Your Pet*. St. Paul, MN: Llewellyn Publications, 2002.

Weschcke, Carl Llewellyn, and Joe H. Slate. *The Llewellyn Complete Book of Psychic Empowerment: A Compendium of Tools & Techniques for Growth & Transformation*. Woodbury, MN: Llewellyn Publications, 2011.

Woodhouse, Barbara. *No Bad Dogs: The Woodhouse Way*. New York: Simon & Schuster, 1984.

INDEX

Allport, Gordon, 16

Asperger's syndrome, 44

auditory, 28, 29, 31, 34, 51–54

Avraamides, Leonidas, 86, 87

Barrett, William, 85, 125

Beard, George M., 138

Bekhterev, Vladimir M., 166

Belly Talk 1, 133

Belly Talk 2, 133

Berger, Hans, 65

Besant, Malcolm, 183

Bishop, Washington Irving, 1, 137, 147

body language, 3, 6, 25, 26, 39–41, 50, 62, 132,
    176, 205

Boone, J. Allen, 164, 172, 173, 179

Braud, William, 126

Breathing, 28, 69, 72, 75, 90, 124, 131, 140, 173,
    198, 199, 201, 203, 206, 207

Brooch or Necklace Effect, 148

Brown, John R., 137, 164

Carington, Whately, 118, 119

Carrington, Hereward, 212

Casas, Isabel, 182

chakra, 183, 207

Chair Test, 142

Color Test, 177

Come to Me, 174, 202

Community of Sensation Test, 125

contact mind reading, 6, 135, 137, 138, 140,
    146, 147, 150, 156, 159

Coover, John E., 94

Crookes, Sir William, 10

Cumberland, Stuart, 137

Darwin, Charles, 1

Daily Routine Exercise, 78

Democritus, 185

dice, 6, 89, 117, 118

"Do You Love Me?" Test, 171

Drawing Experiment, 78

Drawing Test, 150

drawings, 6, 65, 78, 79, 115, 118, 119, 150, 154

dreams, 6, 63, 126, 127, 179, 181–191,
    197, 209, 210

Drink Test, 120

Duke University, 92, 94, 174

Dundas, Joy, 11

Durov, Vladimir, 166, 167

Ehrenwald, Jan, 10

Eisenberg, Nancy, 40

E-Mail Test, 89

Emerson, Ralph Waldo, 51

energy, 3, 5, 25, 34–37, 66, 71–76, 130, 183,
    195, 203, 207

Energy Transfer Exercise, 74

ESP cards, 6, 92–94, 96, 98, 108–111, 115, 118

eye patterns, 51–53

Eye Test, 81

eyes, 5, 20, 29, 32, 37, 40, 42–56, 58–60, 69, 70,
    72, 75, 76, 81, 90, 124, 128, 129, 131, 133,
    138, 140, 142, 152, 154, 157, 167, 169, 171–174,
    183, 184, 189, 191, 196–203, 206–208

facial expressions, 3, 37, 39–41, 56, 159, 205

Family Telepathy, 79

Fifty-fifty, 98, 99, 117, 155

Finding a Hidden Object, 144

Finding a Person, 145, 146

Finding a Playing Card, 145, 146

Finding a Playing Card Variation, 146

Finding an Object, 137, 143, 144

Faraday, Ann, 188

Food Bowl Test, 174

Four Boxes, 122, 123

Freed, William, 11, 12

Freud, Sigmund, 10, 181, 211, 212

ganzfeld experiments, 6, 126–129, 131, 132

Garrett, Eileen, 95, 111, 212

Gladstone, William, 10

Goldberg, Lewis, 16

Grateful Dead, 183

Guessing Game, 155, 156

Haggard, H. Rider, 190, 191

Hand on Head Test, 80

haragei, 6, 132–135

Hardy, Sir Alister, 163

Hearts, Clubs, Spades, or Diamonds, 103

Hellstrom, Axel, 137

Hidden Ring, 148

Honorton, Charles, 126, 127, 183

Horoscope Sign, 146

How to Send Love to Someone, 206

How to Transmit a Thought to Someone
    Who Is Sleeping, 184

Hugo, Victor, 42

Hunter, Fay, 11

Husband and Wife, 35, 149

Huxley, Aldous, 10

Ickes, William, 205

Initial Telepathy Exercise, 76

Institute of Noetic Sciences, 5

Invisible Picture, 123

James, William, 51

Journey reading, 198, 204

kinesthetic, 28–31, 34, 51, 53, 54

Kreskin, 150

Krippner, Stanley, 183, 187

Lawrence, Mimi, 10, 165

Leontovich, Alexander, 166

LeShan, Lawrence, 10

Lie Detector, 106

Linzmayer, Adam, 108

Livingstone, David, 182

Locating a Book, 146

lucid dreams, 188, 189

Maimonides Dream Laboratory, 126, 127, 181,
    183, 187

Mangan, G. L., 121

McDougall, William, 94

Mehrabian, Albert, 41

Metzger, Wolfgang, 126

mirroring, 25, 26, 28

Myers, Frederic, 9

Noncontact Touch Experiment, 159

Onassis, Aristotle, 43

One in Fifty, 116, 117

One in Five, 106, 115, 116

One in Six, 118

One to Ten, 74, 104

One Red Card, 104

One Week Test, 87

Osis, Karlis, 174, 175

Painful Experiment, 125

Parker, Adrian, 126

Party Games, 155

Pearce, Hubert, 108, 109

Perez, Rafael, 182

Perkins, Hugh, 165, 166

Persinger, Michael, 187

pets, 161, 164–166, 171, 176

photographs, 6, 78, 114–118, 124, 127–132, 153,
    154, 184

Playfair, Guy Lyon, 151, 152

playing cards, 6, 92–94, 98–100, 103, 104, 106, 109,
    110, 118, 121

Please Call Me, 90

Power of Emotions, 154

Priestley, J. B., 2

probability, 98, 99

Process of Elimination, 107

pupils, 42–44, 46

Pure Telepathy, 97, 116

Questions and Answers, 175

Quotes and Jokes, 122

Rao, K. Ramakrishna, 120

rapid eye movement, 183, 189

rapport, 5, 13, 21, 23–26, 28, 30, 31, 34, 37,
    55, 76, 196

Red or Black, 98, 99, 101, 103

Remote Experiment, 171

Rhine, J. B., 11, 92–97, 108, 109, 113, 118,
    165, 174

Rings on Her Fingers, 149

Rivers, Olivia, 11

Robichon, Fabrice-Henri, 97, 98

Rumi, 197

Same or Different, 153

Sending Love and Friendship to Strangers, 209

Sensitivity Exercise with a Partner, 36

Shackleton, Basil, 95

Shared Dream Experiment, 187

sheep-goat effect, 96

Sheldrake, Rupert, 83, 86–88, 157–159, 164, 166

Schmeidler, Gertrude, 96

Sherman, Harold, 63, 64

Side Visit, 178

Sinclair, Upton, 118

Smedley, Jenny, 165

Society for Psychical Research, 9, 10, 12, 85, 95,
    96, 110, 164, 174, 182, 187, 191

Solo Sensitivity Exercise, 35

Stanford University, 94

Stanley, Sir Henry Morton, 182, 183, 187

Stekel, Wilhem, 185, 186

Sway Test, 157

synchronized breathing, 28

Telepathic Postman, 148

telepathy, 2, 3, 5, 6, 9–11, 13, 14, 20, 21, 63, 64, 66,
    73, 74, 76–79, 83–88, 90–93, 96–99, 103, 104, 111,
    112, 115, 116, 118, 120, 125, 126, 128, 137, 143,
    148, 151, 155, 158, 159, 163–170, 172–179, 181–187,
    190–193, 195, 196, 207–211

Telephone Test, 88, 89

Telephone Test Variation, 89

Ten Times Five, 105

Ten to Ninety-Nine, 154

Tennyson, Lord, 10

Thorssen, Linda, 176

Thoughts of Food Experiment, 173

Twain, Mark, 10, 84, 85

twins, 11, 98, 125

Ullman, Montague, 181, 183

Vasiliev, Leonid L., 10, 117

visual, 28–31, 34, 41, 51–56, 102

Wallace, Alfred Russel, 125

Warm-up Exercise, 72, 74

Where Is It?, 130, 178

Wilberforce, Bishop Samuel, 1, 2

Wilkins, Sir Hubert, 63, 64

Willing Game, 155, 156

Wiseman, Richard, 155

Wiseman Experiment, 155

Woodhouse, Barbara, 165

Writing a Chosen Word, 149

Young, Terry and Sherry, 11, 20, 24, 52, 165, 187, 209

Zener, Karl, 94, 108

To Write to the Author

If you wish to contact the author or would like more information about this book, please write to the author in care of Llewellyn Worldwide Ltd. and we will forward your request. Both the author and publisher appreciate hearing from you and learning of your enjoyment of this book and how it has helped you. Llewellyn Worldwide Ltd. cannot guarantee that every letter written to the author can be answered, but all will be forwarded. Please write to:

Richard Webster
℅ Llewellyn Worldwide
2143 Wooddale Drive
Woodbury, MN 55125-2989

Please enclose a self-addressed stamped envelope for reply,
or $1.00 to cover costs. If outside the U.S.A., enclose
an international postal reply coupon.

Many of Llewellyn's authors have websites with additional information and resources. For more information, please visit our website at
http://www.llewellyn.com.